LOWDOWN FROM THE LESSON TEE

Correcting 40 of Golf's Most Misunderstood Teaching Tips

David Glenz

1998 PGA National Teacher of the Year

with John J. Monteleone

 **A Mountain Lion Book**

Contemporary Books

Chicago   New York   San Francisco   Lisbon   London   Madrid   Mexico City
Milan   New Delhi   San Juan   Seoul   Singapore   Sydney   Toronto

Library of Congress Cataloging-in-Publication Data

Glenz, David.
    Lowdown from the lesson tee : correcting 40 of golf's most misunderstood
teaching tips / by David Glenz with John J. Monteleone.
        p.   cm.
    Includes index.
    ISBN 0-8092-9618-7 (acid-free paper)
    1. Golf—Study and teaching.   I. Monteleone, John J.   II. Title.

GV962.5.G54   2001
796.352'3—dc21   2001017361

Contemporary Books

A Division of The **McGraw·Hill** *Companies*

1 2 3 4 5 6 7 8 9 0 VL/VL 0 9 8 7 6 5 4 3 2 1

ISBN 0-8092-9618-7

Printed and bound by Vicks Litho

Cover design by Nick Panos
Interior design by Max Crandall
Photos taken by Mike Plunkett

McGraw-Hill books are available at special quantity discounts to use as premiums and
sales promotions, or for use in corporate training programs. For more information, please
write to the Director of Special Sales, Professional Publishing, McGraw-Hill, Two Penn
Plaza, New York, NY 10121-2298. Or contact your local bookstore.

This book is printed on acid-free paper.

CONTENTS

ACKNOWLEDGMENTS

The purpose of this book is to enlighten the readers with information I have learned throughout my career in golf. A special thanks to:

- my parents, Lloyd and Peggy, who introduced me to golf at age nine. I wish they were still around to enjoy the book.
- my first instructor, Al Williams, for all the time he spent with me.
- Johnny Revolta and Bob Toski, for the help they gave me during my playing days. Not only did Bob help me as a player but he was also a great inspiration as a teacher.
- Jim MacLean, with whom I played a lot of golf, competing and exchanging ideas on the golf swing as we advanced in teaching.

A very special thanks to all my students and my teaching staff. I still learn daily from my staff and from the students we teach. Certainly, without the help and expertise of John Monteleone, this book would never have gotten off the ground. Thanks again, John.

• • •

This book was conceived, developed, and produced by Mountain Lion, Inc., a book packager specializing in instructional and general reference sports books. A book packager relies on the special skills of many people. The following contributed to the production of *Lowdown from the Lesson Tee*. To each of them we say thank you.

Rob Taylor, acquiring editor at Contemporary Books, whose laser-like long irons are always struck dead solid perfect, and whose imagination helped shaped this book.

Mark Gola, managing editor and aspiring player, who selected the photographs as well as modeled for the jacket cover photographs.

Michael Plunkett, photographer, who when he broke from regaling all with reports of his most recent legendary round of bogie-free golf took all the still and sequence photography.

INTRODUCTION

Over the nearly thirty years I've spent as a golf instructor I've encountered many golf instruction expressions and phrases that have brought as much harm as good to aspiring players. My students brought some of them to me. Others I discovered along the way from fellow competitors, clinics, books, magazines, and videotape. You too, I'm sure, have encountered these phrases, these nuggets of fool's gold, such as "Swing the same on all shots" and "Keep your head still." Unfortunately, these "truisms" often stir up the wrong interpretations, generate faulty connotations, and generally lead players who are trying to improve down the wrong path.

Until now, with the writing of this book, these expressions have generally gone unquestioned. On the following pages I will explore forty of golf's most misinterpreted and misunderstood teaching tips. You will gain a better understanding of what the originator of the phrase or advice was really intending to impart. You will learn the shortcomings and, if applicable, the relative merits of each tenet, as some only lack a clear and proper interpretation to be helpful. However, those that truly mislead, will be carefully amended and/or summarily declared out-of-bounds (O.B.). In the case of the latter, I will provide alternative advice and instruction.

These clarifications, corrections, reinterpretations, and amplifications will draw heavily from my own teaching methods and ideas. I will discuss the basic elements of the swing. However, my teaching concepts on the golf swing, which are very simple and straightforward, focus on two important aspects: (1) the positioning and movement of the body and (2) a simple, direct movement of the clubhead. The most important things you will learn about the structure and movement of the body are how to set up with good structure and how to move the body back behind the ball and then into and through it. It's simple and easy to learn and you won't get twisted up like Chubby Checker. I guarantee it!

My teaching on club movement focuses on (1) moving the clubhead directly away from the ball with the clubface looking at the ball, that is, square to the target line, (2) bending the right wrist backward in a natural loading action, and (3) returning the clubhead into and through the ball, the right wrist fully unloading and right hand freely smacking the ball away toward the target. As you might guess, you will learn how important I believe the hands are in the golf swing.

You may use this book as the need arises. It is divided so that you can turn directly to the subject of pressing interest. Sections of this book dealing with the basic swing mechanics, such as the backswing, forward swing and impact, should be read, thought about, tried and practiced, and then reread. By returning to the text and photographs for further study, you will begin to cultivate and eventually ingrain the motor skills necessary for mastering the aspect of golf that is of most concern to you.

This book will not only teach you a lot about the proper way to swing a golf club but it will help you better evaluate and/or eliminate invalid ideas and replace them with more useful ones. It will help to hit the ball more consistently, it will help you putt better, and of course it will help you become an overall better player, which is why I believe you're holding this book in your hands.

Grip, Stance, and Setup

● **No. 1**

Grip the club like you're holding a bird

> *The basic factor in all good golf is the grip. Get it right, and all other progress follows.*
>
> — Tommy Armour

Finding the right amount of grip pressure when holding the golf club is important but I don't believe this particular bit of advice is very useful. You may have heard another similar tip, "Grip the club as if you're holding an open tube of toothpaste without squeezing any paste out the end."

If you follow either of these instructions you will simply not have enough pressure to control the club. On a scale of 1 to 10, with 10 being the firmest grip possible, gripping a club like holding a bird would be at pressure level 1. This is not firm enough, especially for women whose hand strength is weaker.

Grip pressure is somewhat subjective. And there is tremendous variation in the amount of hand pressure among players. However, no one can hold the club at level 1 or level 10 and expect to perform well—the extremes don't work. When you hold the club too loosely, you lose control of the clubhead. When you grip the club too tightly you diminish the sense of feel; that is, you lose a sense of where the club is, in what direction the face is pointed, and other critical feedback.

*You can fake about anything, but a bad grip
will follow you to the grave.*

— Gary McCord

Here's how to find hand pressure that will allow you to control the club without creating excessive tension that comes from death grips on the club handle.

Finding the right pressure

1. Hold a club parallel to the ground, arms slightly bent. If you slacken the pressure to level 1, as if you had a bird in your hands, the clubhead drops. If you squeeze the handle as tight as possible, your forearms, wrists, and fingers create tension. You soon lose a feeling for the head of the club, which will lead to trouble because you need to feel the clubhead to sense where it is when you swing.

Hold the club parallel to the ground (1). You should be able to feel the head. When you slacken the tension of the grip too much, the clubhead drops (2). Holding the club too loosely diminishes control of the clubhead.

2. Reduce the pressure until the clubhead falls slightly. Regrip until it sta-bilizes. Move the clubhead up, down, and side-to-side without fully con-tracting the forearms and without causing your knuckles to turn white. This is the correct feeling, the correct amount of grip pressure for you. Make a mental note of where it falls on the scale of 1 to 10. You're probably above 3 and below 8—and you're in control of the clubhead without tension.

> *Quiet hands respond on their own to the weight*
> *of the clubhead. Tight hands have to be told*
> *what to do.*
>
> — *Jim Flick*

A second check to determine if you have the correct grip pressure is to hold the club in the left hand (bottom hand for a right-handed player) across the heel pad, then lift it without losing control. Then grip the club with the right hand only and lift it without losing control. Next, put both hands on the club and lift. This should lighten the pressure slightly—and equally—in each hand.

Make yourself conscious of this—going from a 6 or 5 pressure rating with one hand to a 5 or 4 with both hands. Remember: (1) whatever your grip pressure, it should be equal in each hand; (2) players who have the right amount of pressure have a feeling of "soft hands" and "passive hands" but not loose hands.

Another way of thinking about this is that proper grip pressure is the lightest possible without loss of control of the club. Any slight increases of pressure come as a response to keeping control of the clubhead as it moves throughout the swing.

Signs of too much pressure

One way to determine if you're applying too much pressure is to examine your hands to see if you're building up excessive callouses, or hardened skin, on your hands. The heel pad and palm area just below the last three digits on the left hand (bottom hand) and just the below the middle two digits of the right hand (top hand) contact the shaft when hand pressure is applied. Check for an excessive buildup of hardened skin, or blisters developed when beginning to play after a layoff from playing. These are sure signs of too much grip pressure or a change of hand pressure during the swing.

Too much grip pressure inhibits the hinging and unhinging of the wrists, which makes it difficult to square the clubhead at impact.

> *You get rewarded at the bottom end of the club*
> *by what you do at the top end.*
>
> — *Jerry Barber*

Watch out in the short game

Be careful with the short game swing that requires you to reduce the pressure and role of the top hand. When you weaken the top hand—that is, place it more on top of the club, thumb turned toward the target, and reduce the grip pressure—you lose the feel of the clubhead and control of your shots. Do not change your hand position or weaken the grip pressure. It doesn't make sense to weaken the right hand when we know that it contributes more of the feel in short game chips. Keep the hand pressure equal, regardless of what pressure level you're gripping the club with.

Avoiding tension

Tension destroys swings. You must find ways to minimize tension and promote what Sam Snead termed an "oily" athletic motion. When hitting full shots, you can use a waggle, a short back-and-forth movement of the club along the line of your intended backswing.

Here's another simple preswing technique, or routine, that minimizes tension:

1. Put one hand on the club, keeping the club at the address position. Look at the target, then back to the ball.
2. Add the other hand and in one continuous motion start the swing. This keeps tension out of the swing because you have no time to build excessive grip pressure. Simply think "Go" as you add the second hand to the grip.

If you practice chipping with the right hand only, you will find the proper pressure for controlling the clubhead and maintaining feel. When you add the left hand, keep its pressure the same as that of the right hand.

When putting you can apply a tension-reducing technique used by baseball players when batting—milking the handle. This is the repetitive lifting and replacing of the fingers on the grip. It prevents the buildup of tension while preparing to stroke the ball.

Another tension reducer is tapping the putter head two or three times and then immediately going into your stroke.

Drill

Here is a drill to help you establish proper grip pressure. Match or align the leading edge of the clubhead to the palm of the right hand, that is, set the clubhead parallel to the plane formed by the plane of the palm. This should be square to the target, perpendicular to the target line. The handle should rest across the first joint of the index finger and under the heel pad, making a 45-degree angle across the hand. Practice chipping with the right hand only. You will find the proper pressure for controlling the clubhead and maintaining feel. When you add the left hand, make sure its pressure is equal to that of the right hand.

● No. 2

When holding the club, apply pressure with the last three fingers of the bottom hand and middle two fingers of the top hand

The key thought of pulling down on the club with last two fingers of the left hand helps prevent the right hand from assuming command and throwing the club from the top.

— Sam Snead

What's going on here? Many instructors and great players have advocated adding some amount of pressure with the last digits of the left hand. Ben Hogan stressed the idea of adding hand pressure with the last three fingers of the bottom hand. I believe he did this because he wanted to engage the muscles that run along the inside of the left forearm, which then provide a heightened feeling of control when squaring the clubhead in the downswing. This couldn't be detrimental, could it?

I don't think so, but Hogan—along with many others who've stressed this—fails to mention other important pressure points that aid in controlling the clubhead. You should also keep pressure on (1) the left-hand thumb against the lifeline of the right-hand palm (the left-hand thumb fits in the lifeline of the right-hand palm) and (2) along the first and second knuckle joints of the right-hand index finger where it presses against the handle. If you do not apply constant pressure with this part of the index finger you risk losing control of the club at the top of the backswing and at impact.

With your overall grip pressure, think of it this way—the fingers hold the club against the palms of the hands, the shaft rests not in the middle of the palms but in the upper pads of the palms toward the base of the fingers. The hands should feel as if they oppose each

Keep pressure against the shaft with the first and second knuckles of the right-hand index finger.

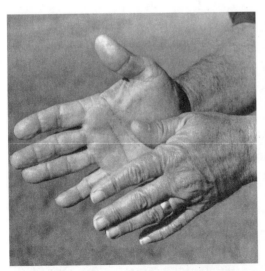
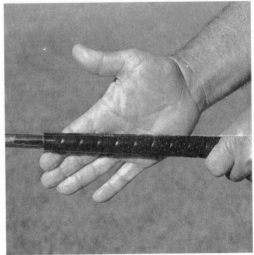

Left: Maintain pressure with the left thumb against the lifeline of the right-hand palm.
Right: The fingers of the hands wrap around the shaft and then press the shaft against the palms. This promotes control of the hands' hinging and unhinging action in the swing.

THINKING PRESSURE UNDER PRESSURE

In his march to the 1982 U.S. Open Championship, Tom Watson used a near-miraculous chip-in at Pebble Beach's no. 17, par-three hole. According to Watson, the shot was made by concentrating hand pressure on the last three fingers of his left hand. Thus, this idea can be a helpful swing-thought in executing a difficult chip shot—for one, it helps to prevent the clubface from closing when playing out of heavy rough.

Watson hits chip shots from the rough with either a sand or pitching wedge and plays them out of the rough in much the same way he plays sand shots. He places the ball at least in the middle of his stance, opens his setup and clubface, and then takes the club up more abruptly on the backswing by hinging the right hand sooner. This avoids catching the club in the grass on the takeaway.

On the forward swing Watson slides the clubhead under the ball with the face held firmly open by the last three fingers of the left hand.

"I can even hit slightly behind the ball, as if I were in the sand, with good results," says Watson.

other—the right hand slightly pushing against the left hand, and vice versa. The hands do not wrap the clubshaft in the deepest part of the palms; rather they press the club against the palms. This promotes control of the hands' hinging and unhinging action in the swing (they must hinge in the backswing and then unhinge in the downswing to square the clubface at impact).

The palms should oppose each other and align parallel to the leading edge of the clubface. If you match your palms with the leading edge of the clubface at address you will get a sense of what "square" is. For one, make sure the right-hand palm is set at 90 degrees to the target line, and the clubface is parallel to the imaginary line formed by the palm.

What about the fingers we haven't mentioned—the little finger of the right hand and the index finger of the left hand—which are either interlocked or overlapped (Vardon grip), thus unifying the hands into one solid grip. What are their roles? Are they more passive than the other fingers? Not at all. When applied correctly, they too are pressing firmly against the club handle as well as against each other.

Thus, I believe that proper grip requires more than pressing the club handle at certain "hot spots." Rather, proper grip pressure is achieved when it's evenly applied along the handle wherever the fingers and palms come into contact.

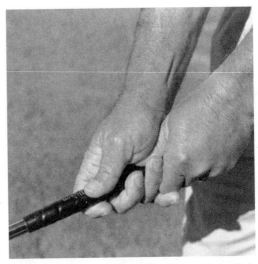

Proper pressure is achieved when it's evenly applied wherever the fingers and palms contact the shaft.

Building awareness
of pressure

Here is a way to build awareness of proper pressure. Place a piece of two-sided adhesive tape on the left-hand thumb where it presses against the right-hand palm (along the lifeline). This will help you get used to the feeling of the hands working together as a unit and sense the appropriate amount of pressure between them.

● **No. 3**

Align your feet parallel to the target line

Much is made of how to aim. Take your stance and hold a clubshaft along the front of your thighs. Look where the club is pointing, and you will see where you are aimed. Laying a club on the ground at your feet will tell you very little.

— Harvey Penick

Getting your feet aligned is a very good idea. But, as Harvey Penick knew, you need more than your feet aligned parallel to the target line. So the problem with this axiom is that its advice really doesn't go as far as it should. To repeat, what we want is the entire body aligned, not just the feet.

In fact, many players have stances that position their feet slightly open (front foot is turned a little off the target line to the left) or closed (rear foot is pulled back away from the target line, leaving the front foot closer), but the rest of the body is aligned parallel. Ben Hogan swung along the line of his body but he varied his stance. When he hit longer clubs he pulled his rear foot away from the target line.

Watch a good player when he hits a short iron, that is, a sand wedge, lob wedge, pitching wedge, or 9 iron. He will pull his front foot slightly away from the target line but keep his chest and hips square, or parallel to the target line.

> *If you haven't had any instruction, it's almost certain that the first things you presently position are your feet, plonking them down in what you hope are the right locations, followed by the clubhead. Break that habit as fast as you can. Because you must align everything else relative to where it faces, always—repeat, always—aim the clubhead first.*
>
> **— John Jacobs**

Align yourself parallel to the target line

I recommend that you align the top of the thighs, hips, knees, shoulders, chest, and feet. Keep them parallel. If you were to place rods across your thighs and chest they should point down the line, parallel to the target line. If you are not properly aligned, they would point to the left or right and form an imaginary line that is not parallel to the target line.

Of all the body parts, it is most important that you align the chest facing the golf ball and parallel to the target line. Swing problems quickly arise when you fail to do so. If you turn the chest too much to the left of the target line,

Proper alignment includes the chest, hips, thighs, and knees. If you were to place a rod across your chest, thighs, or knees it would point down the line, parallel to the target line. Of all the body parts, it is most important that you align the chest (2) facing the golf ball and parallel to the target line.

which is a common problem in faulty alignments, you will fail to keep the club in front of your body as you begin the coil in the backswing. This sequence error gets the club behind the body going away so the body has to wait on the through swing for the hands and club to catch up. The result is a brownout in your power. You'll hit shots less solidly and with less carry and roll.

Keep your eyes on the target as you set your feet

You must use your eyes constantly in setting up to hit the ball. First, sight your target line from the target back to the ball. Visualize the flight of the shot. Approach the side of the ball so that an imaginary line from your sternum to the target line would form a perpendicular angle (90 degrees). Your chest is now parallel to the target line. Aim the clubface at your target, then set your feet, take one or two glances at the target, moving your head only. This will help you to maintain your chest in a square position and prevent your feet from moving off a line parallel to the target line.

Correct alignment is not like riding a bicycle.
You can forget. You can slip into bad habits.

— Jim Flick

Checking your alignment

Here's how to check that your chest alignment is correctly positioned. Assume your stance, then place a clubshaft across your chest. Where does it point? If it points either left or right of a line parallel to the target line, making an angle with the target line, you're not aligned correctly. You've positioned your chest open too much (pointing to the left) or closed too much (pointing to the right). Adjust accordingly until your club is parallel to the target line.

A quick way of checking alignment during a round is to look down at your knees as you set up in your stance. If you are in good position, you'll see the same amount of shoe tops on each side. If either one of the tops of your knees hides more of your ankle and shoe, your chest is not parallel to the target line. If more of your right shoe is covered from view, you have turned your chest (and hips) too far to the left. If too much of the top of your left foot is hidden from view, you've turned too far to the right.

HITTING THE DRAW AND FADE

When is a square or parallel setup a detriment to the shot you're trying to hit? When you're hitting a fade or draw. To hit a fade, a shot that curves from left to right, set the clubface aimed at the target but your body—shoulders, hips, knees—aimed to the left of it. Swing the club along your body lines. To curve a ball from right to left, that is, to hit a draw, aim your body lines to the right of the target while leaving the clubface aimed at the target. Swing the club along your body lines.

Remember: (1) these shots do not require you to make any adjustments to your grip and (2) the less loft you are using, the easier it is to curve the ball. With a fade, the ball will fly shorter and higher than a straight shot and will run less when it hits the ground. With a draw, the ball will fly lower than a straight shot and once it hits the ground will run more.

Ball position is a critical factor in maintaining the body's parallel lines. When you move the ball forward in your stance, that is, from opposite your sternum toward the left heel (for a right-handed player), the chest tends to open, or point to the left of parallel. Check for this. Keep it square or parallel to the target line.

If on certain holes you go out of bounds or into water or rough so much you think you are jinxed, why don't you try checking your stance? Place the club at the tips of your toes and often you'll be amazed to learn that you actually are aiming at trouble.

— Tommy Armour

No. 4
Place your feet shoulder-width apart

When you stand to the ball your hips should be bending forward at approximately twenty degrees. Your rear end should be stuck out and up a little bit but not too much. It should feel like a ready athletic position, as if you were standing to field a ground ball or shoot a free throw.

— Hank Haney

The correct setup position of the feet is for the inside of your feet to be situated just outside the edges of the hips. The feet must be wide enough to contain the lateral movement in the golf swing. When the body moves lat-

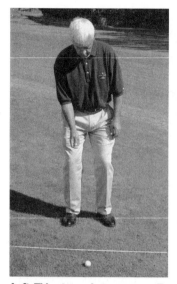  

Left: This stance is too narrow. To set up with the proper stance width (*center and right*), make sure your feet are wide enough to contain the lateral movement of the golf swing. The inside of your feet must be situated just outside the edges of the hips.

erally and coils, the weight must be contained inside the legs. When you move too far—that is, you allow your weight to roll onto the outside of your right foot—you create instability. The body sways and creates all kinds of problems. Among other things it moves the bottom of your swing to a spot behind the ball, thus causing you to hit "fat" shots (when the clubface contacts the ground an inch or so behind the ball).

The correct position at address is often referred to as the "athletic position" because it approximates the position that athletes assume when playing other sports, such as the position that a basketball player takes when guarding an opponent who has the ball, or the position that a baseball player takes when batting or getting ready to field a ground ball. It is a position that allows for an explosive but controlled movement of the entire body, such as shuffling, jumping, turning, pivoting, diving, or running. In golf, the "athletic" movements are coiling, loading the weight on the right leg, and firing the backside into and through the ball, down the target line.

A good rule of thumb when determining the width of what would be an athletic stance is that it should be wide enough to enable you to maintain good balance yet narrow enough so you can move freely into the back leg on the backswing and unwind fully around the front leg on the through swing. A stance that is too wide will restrict rotational movement of the body. A stance that is too narrow will tend to cause swaying and other excessive lateral lower body movement. However, the width of your stance should vary according to the club you are using and the aggressiveness of the motion. With shorter clubs, you can slightly narrow your stance. With wedges, you can also pull your left foot slightly away from the target line, thus making it easier to release the back side into the shot.

To check to see if you're in an athletic posture, jump in the air. You won't get airborne without it.

Drill

Check your stance by looking at the inside of the feet. The back foot must be positioned outside the back hip. For the athletic feel, jump in the air from your golf posture. This will give you the feel of the weight being evenly distributed on both feet and the legs feeling springy rather than tight and flexed.

CLOSED VERSUS OPEN STANCE

When the feet are equidistant from the target line, you're in a square stance. This gives you enough freedom for a full backswing and a freewheeling forward swing. The closed stance, when the right foot is farther from the target line than the left foot, somewhat restricts body rotation on the forward swing. The open stance, when the left foot is farther from the target line than the right foot, restricts body coil in the backswing but allows you to better unwind on the forward swing. A slightly open stance is the preferred setup when using wedges and short irons on approach shots to the green. At address the back foot should be placed perpendicular to the target—the foot position advocated and preferred by Ben Hogan—or slightly splayed open. Point the front foot open to the target at least 15 degrees. This makes unwinding of the body through the ball much easier.

● No. 5

Flex the legs at address

> *I have the feeling when I'm taking my stance
> that someone has just pulled a chair from behind
> me and I'm waiting for him to put it back.*
>
> — *Arnold Palmer*

Flexing the legs is good advice because it's important that you get into an athletic stance in the setup. However, this directive often leads players into problems. How much flex? Bend the knees only? Bend at the waist? I've seen the advice go wrong when a player does not flex in the proper sequence or the proper amount. If you first flex the legs, and then bend at the waist, you've got problems.

You should first tilt the spine forward from the hips. The hips should move back and the legs should relax to center the weight athletically over the feet.

The spine should be positioned 90 degrees to the clubshaft. An imaginary extension of the clubshaft would run through the body and intersect with the small of the back. Remember, when you flex the legs after tilting forward from the hips, you allow for taking the proper angle of the spine.

At address tilt the spine forward from the hips. Move the hips back and relax the legs, centering the weight athletically over the feet.

When you flex the legs first and then bend forward from the waist you tend to create a spine angle that is rounded and too vertical in relation to the club. And you lose balance because your upper body tends to rest slightly back in the heels. The legs flex too much and build too much tension.

Too much leg flex causes the knees to sway during the swing. The knees must work within the confines of the body as the legs support the rotating movement of the body into the back leg and into and around the front leg. Too much leg flex creates lateral instability in the lower body. This not only feels awkward but it also creates tension in the legs and fatigue.

Most of the things that contribute to a bad shot in golf occur before you begin your backswing.

— Jim Flick

Testing for proper weight distribution

Here is a simple test to determine if your weight is properly distributed at address. Assume what you consider is a proper address position. Now jump in the air. If your weight is pitched too far forward you will lose balance and tend to fall over to the front. If your weight is resting too much on the heels you won't be able to get airborne at all. If your weight is evenly distributed and centered you will roll up slightly on the balls of your feet, elevate and return to the same place without losing balance. This is the value of assuming the athletic position at address.

When you flex your legs first, you will not be able to fully coil and uncoil. Your entire body will be too low. Lowering the body might be good for hitting a shot from a difficult lie that is several inches below your feet, such as hitting a sand bunker shot with your feet

To check for proper weight distribution jump in the air. If it is evenly distributed and centered, you will return to the same place.

outside the bunker and the ball in it, but it won't work when hitting normal shots.

Another poor result from this stance is that your head goes down too far at address. It restricts a free body rotation on both the backswing and forward swing. With your head in the way, your body cannot rotate fully and freely in the backswing, a flaw that leads to a shortened swing and a shutdown of power.

Too many people, I believe, feel so uncomfortable and off balance at address that it's almost impossible for them to get the swing started, let alone finish it.

— Mickey Wright

Checking your posture at address

Here is an easy way to check your posture at address. Stand erect and hold an old clubshaft, sawed-off broomstick handle, or rod down your spine. It should touch the tailbone, middle of the back, and your head. Tilt the spine forward, keeping your back, head, and spine in contact with rod or clubshaft. Notice how the hips naturally move back, keeping the tailbone in contact with the rod, as you tilt and the legs naturally relax to center the weight on the feet.

If you practice in front of a mirror you can check the stance by looking at the angle created by the natural line of the spine and the clubshaft. Properly positioned, the angle should be 90 degrees. Improperly positioned—too far bent over—the angle will be less than 90 degrees. Not tilted enough, the angle will be more than 90 degrees at setup. This causes the flaw of working the club too much around the body.

Check your posture at address. Stand erect and hold an old clubshaft down your spine (1).
Notice how the hips naturally move back, keeping the tailbone in contact with the rod (2).

Practice setup with different clubs

Practice your setup with a short iron, medium iron, and wood. Notice how the hands move away from the body as the clubs get longer and the spine tilts less. However, the intersection of the clubshaft with the body is always 90 degrees and it always runs through the small of the back.

● # No. 6

Set up so that the left arm and clubshaft form a straight line

"Keep your left arm straight" is a myth. It's more important to keep your muscles free from tension. Loose muscles let you make a bigger turn and swing the club faster.

— Gale Peterson

This is another misconception that arises from looking at the setup, especially for the driver, at a face-front angle. Often, when we view a setup from the face-on, the left arm appears to form a straight line from the shoulder and down the clubshaft to the ball. However, if you look at the setup and alignment from behind and down the target line you'll see that the hands and arms hang under the shoulders and form an angle with the clubshaft.

Stiffen versus straight

Extension of the left arm during the backswing lengthens your swing arc and stretches the left side; and the bigger your swing arc and the more stretch, the faster the clubhead moves. However, in striving to keep the left arm straight, some golfers stiffen it; that is, they tighten the muscles all the way up to the shoulder socket, including the left side of the torso, wrist, and hand, and lock the left elbow. This results in too much tension, which restricts upper-body coiling and prevents the body from completely stretching away from the ball. Additionally, the right hand and arm seldom get in a proper loaded position, a critical aspect of a powerful golf swing.

To reach a full arc with an extended but not stiffened left arm, first relax the left arm and then pull it to full extension with the right hand as you move to the top of the backswing. You can do this without any extra conscious effort by simply bending your right arm at the elbow to 90 degrees—a right angle—or slightly more in the backswing. Try it and you'll find that the left arm extends and straightens without tension. You should also feel a tremendous stretch of the muscles up the left side of the body.

Try a swing without forcing the left arm
straight; it might suit you to bend it a little.

— Henry Cotton

Left: Allow the arms hang down under the shoulder. *Right:* Do not stiffen them or reach them away from the body.

Is the left arm straightened at impact?

Yes. At impact the left arm is fully straightened and the right arm is slightly bent. The left and right arms both straighten to full extension just inches beyond impact. From face-on, you can see that they form a V-shape. Here, the left arm and clubshaft do momentarily form a straight line, the result of centrifugal force, and perfect timing. After impact, the left arm folds as the right arm and wrist rolls over the left arm and the clubhead moves to the left of the target line and back around the body.

Even though the left arm reaches full extension at impact and slightly beyond, you should not set up this way. If you did, you would have an unnaturally stiff arm that would raise the left shoulder and promote a hunched position; that is, the left shoulder would move closer to the target line and slightly higher than desired at address and setup.

One of the enduring myths of golf is that a player's left arm must be straight and fully extended at the top of the backswing. On the contrary, I've found that having a slight flex in the left arm enables a player to generate more leverage to swing the club powerfully . . . for players who want to hit the ball long and hard, the only moment in the swing when the left arm should straighten is at impact.

— *Art Sellinger*

Hands and arms work together

Don't assume that because the left arm has moved to full extension at impact that it is doing more of the work, that is, delivering more of the force that strikes the ball. The right hand and arm are greatly instrumental in generating the power surge. Ben Hogan observed, "When it comes to power I wish I had three right hands."

In the forward swing the body drives into the front foot and leg. This action pulls the hands and arms down into the hitting slot. As the body starts unwinding around the front foot and leg, the right hand fires the clubhead directly back down the target line on approach to impact. The left hand stabilizes the club as the right hand hits full out through impact.

> *It is an invariable rule that if you start the arms—either at the beginning or at the top of the swing—the result is bad.*
>
> *— Harry Vardon*

Drill

Make a right-hand-only backswing. First take the club back 2 feet. Now put the left hand on the club. Both arms are extended at this point. Now take the club back half way with the right hand in a throwing position. Now put your left hand on the club. Notice how the left arm is extended and the left side stretched. Now go to a full throwing position of the right hand (take it back above the right shoulder) and see if you can now reach the club by extending your left arm and stretching your left side. If you've been trying to keep your left arm straight to get to this position, I don't think it felt like this.

PULLING HARD PUTS YOU OVER THE TOP

A misunderstood corollary to keeping your left arm straight is the advice to pull down hard with the left arm. What's really going on here? First, the body moves onto the front leg, to initiate the downswing. Then, as the left side unwinds, it creates a pulling action that runs through the left arm. But be careful not to exaggerate this pulling action and force the swing away from your body on the downswing. A hard pulling action of the left arm and shoulder create the classic "over the top" downswing. A downward pulling of the left arm jams the arms into the body, creating a body response of pulling up and away through impact. The body cannot uncoil properly and this will block the release of the right side, which must move past the ball down the target line after impact.

The proper swing requires the coordination of both sides of the body. Each contributes to the proper swing, taking over at different times. The left side leads the downswing, uncoiling and pulling the left arm into the hitting area. Your left arm moves toward full extension at the very bottom of the swing. The right side moves into action about halfway through the downswing when the hands are about waist high. The right hand fires the clubhead down and along the swing path into and through the back of the ball.

No. 7
Position the ball opposite your left heel

The only time your hands should be to the right of the ball at address is when you are addressing a teed-up drive that you will catch on the upswing. Your hands should be ahead of the ball at address for all other shots because you are going to hit those shots on the downswing.

— Tommy Armour

Many players, even Tour players, play the ball too close to their front foot. Jack Nicklaus and Ben Hogan wrote about hitting the ball opposite the left heel but video analysis shows that they hit the ball on most of their shots farther back in the stance.

Hitting the ball opposite the left heel, or closer to the front foot than the back foot, works well when hitting a driver off a tee, but not for much else in the bag. I suspect that this idea continues to confuse players because golf magazines love to feature the driver in swing photography.

Every golfer has one ideal ball position in his stance. Take a swing without a ball, and take a divot. The beginning of the divot indicates where the ball should be positioned.

— Davis Love Jr.

On most shots the last thing you want to do is move the ball too far forward. When you position the ball too far forward you move it forward of the spot that is the natural bottom of your swing. To make contact, you then need excessive lateral movement to make sure you hit the ball before you hit the ground. Even when you do make contact, it's a good news/ bad news situation: balls that are struck (the good news, you managed to make clean contact) too far forward in the setup tend to fly left of the target (the bad news, you're out of bounds or over in the neighboring fairway).

Most golf shots are better off when struck in the center of the stance opposite the sternum.

Minimize lateral movement

Ideally you want the body movement—the slight lateral movement and coiling/uncoiling of the torso—to be contained within the space defined by the feet and legs. To do this, position the ball opposite your sternum. Now, the natural bottom of your swing should be slightly forward of the ball. You should get crisp contact with a clubface square to the target line.

How to check for proper ball position

To check if the ball is positioned properly, pick up the club while at address and move the end of the shaft toward the body. If it touches the sternum or the imaginary line that runs from the top to the bottom of the body through the sternum, then you've positioned the ball properly. Or simply get in front of a mirror on the practice range. Line up and then adjust until the ball is in the center of your body.

After you have established where the center is—opposite the sternum—you can learn to hit a lower shot by moving the ball back slightly, an inch or one-half inch, and you can hit the ball a little higher by moving the ball slightly forward, again only an inch or one-half inch. A caution: the more you move the ball forward, the greater chance that your swing will bottom out prior to impact, thus hitting shots that are either thin (contacting the ball with the leading edge of the clubface) or fat (chunking the club into the turf behind the ball) or pulling the shot to the left of your intended target line.

At address, move the shaft toward your body and make sure it's aligned in the middle of your sternum.

Faulty ball position can lead to injury

Riding forward and then rotating to hit a ball positioned opposite the left heel puts a lot of pressure on the left hip. Over time, this can lead to excessive wear and tear and eventually to debilitating injury. I suspect that some of Jack Nicklaus's hip problems might have resulted from this. If you position the ball too far back, you will tend to hit the ball to the right because the clubface has not had time to release to a square position at impact.

Impact is in a slightly different place for each club; that is, as the ball position varies slightly, so does impact. Players strike the ball with varying degrees of proficiency from these varying ball positions. Some play better from certain positions. For example, hockey players who take up golf are

Impact is in a slightly different place for each club. Play the wedges and short irons (through 7) in the middle of your stance—opposite your sternum—and the woods slightly forward.

excellent at hitting the ball slightly back in their stance. They're accustomed to trapping the puck and sending it low across the ice. In golf, they hit great short irons but they're not as effective with that swing when hitting woods. Every player must adapt the swing to the particular situation—one size does not fit all.

I recommend that you play your wedges and short irons, through the 7 iron, off the middle of your chest. When you're swinging a 6, 5, or 4 iron, move the ball slightly forward, a half inch at the most. Even when hitting the fairway woods, you will be better off placing the ball only slightly forward of your sternum.

A slicer who moves the ball back in his stance (after judging it too far forward) will also have to work on getting his clubhead approaching the ball from the inside track. For the player who is constantly fighting a hook, moving the ball forward in his stance (after finding it too far back) will only help matters if at the same time he is able to work on improving his swing path too, so that the club is more on line as it approaches the ball.

— David Leadbetter

❚❚ Backswing

● **No. 8**

Take the club back low

*The clubhead is kept low as it starts
back from the ball by shifting of
weight laterally from the left foot to
the right foot.*

— Byron Nelson

Taking the club back low, as well as the idea of taking the club back
in one piece, that is, a "one-piece takeaway," certainly has merit.
My quarrel with the advice is that players need to know how far
to keep the takeaway low. And they need to know when the club
must move up, back, and around as the body coils away from the
ball. Without a clear idea of this, the low takeaway can lead to an
overextension of the arms—a definite misinterpretation.

When the hands reach a position opposite the rear leg, as the
clubhead moves to the inside of the target line, the clubhead
should begin to rise. The angle of takeaway will vary with the
club. For example, longer clubs such as fairway woods will remain
low to the ground longer than shorter clubs, such as the pitching
wedge. This is due to the longer shaft and the body's more pro-
nounced move into the back leg.

The club in most cases needs to start moving away from the
ball at a shallow angle. To visualize the arc or angle in the takeaway, think of how a plane lands. It doesn't descend in a steep vertical plane. It glides in at a shallow angle. A key to this movement
is to keep the hands the same distance from the body. To do this,

(1) When the hands reach a position opposite the rear leg, as the clubhead moves to the inside of the target line, the clubhead should begin to rise. At the halfway point (2) the clubshaft is pointed perpendicular to the left arm.

allow your body to move to the back leg and begin coiling, thus avoiding the fault of pushing the club farther along the path of the target line than is necessary, or desirable.

Starting the club back low will help to avoid three troublesome faults that can show up in the backswing: (1) picking the club up, (2) taking the club inside too quickly, and (3) opening the clubface.

Picking the club up and opening the clubface are problems resulting from excessive, independent arm and hand action; they are not working in unison with the body. When you pick the club up abruptly you risk bringing it back on a steep angle, thus shutting down power and increasing the chances of hitting "fat" shots, that is, making contact an inch or two behind the ball. When you open the clubface in the backswing—which can be simply the result of a faulty grip—you then need to manipulate the clubface to bring it back to square as it approaches the ball along the target line.

Bringing the club inside too soon is usually a result of the takeaway coming too much from the left arm or a misinterpretation of the idea of creating a swing path that is "in-to-out." Ironically, if you bring the club back too severely to the inside on the backswing or takeaway, the only way back to the ball is to swing out-to-in. The results are undesirable: either a slice or a pull. Simply keep in mind that once the hands reach the rear leg, the club-head begins to rise. Follow that advice and you'll heighten your chances of hitting your shots long and straight.

The most important single move in establishing your tempo and rhythm is your takeaway. It sets the beat for everything that comes later. Strive on every shot to move the club back as deliberately as possible, consistent with swinging it back rather than taking it back.

— Jack Nicklaus

Left: Practice the takeaway, right hand only. Keep the left arm relaxed over the ball. **Right:** Take the club just past halfway back to a throwing position of the right hand.

A DIFFERENT TAKE

PGA instructor Michael Hebron has an interesting and useful analysis of the takeaway and backswing. He believes that the backswing is only inches long. Which it is, if you measure the distance that the left shoulder moves from setup to the end of the backswing. According to Hebron, while the clubhead has traveled a great distance (about 27 feet), the torso/body has moved only a few inches. Hebron also notes that with most golfers we see a backswing that is too long, and he knows why. He explains, "When you try to swing the club all the way back to the spot we traditionally have accepted as the top or end of the backswing, the club will travel beyond that point because of the laws of physics and momentum."

My experience on the lesson tee has shown that when students are asked to swing the club to what they feel is a one-half-length backswing, most bring the club to parallel. When they properly coil the body, their distance does not suffer from this "at the top" position. Try it in front of a mirror and see if your backswing is too long.

Drill

Take the club back with the right hand only for the first foot. Then put the left hand on the club and see what it feels like. It should feel extended but not too stretched. From this point, remove the left hand and take the club back halfway to a throwing position of the right hand. Practice the takeaway, right hand only, keeping the clubface looking at the ball for the initial 2 feet. What I mean when I say "looking at the ball" is keeping the clubface square to the target line (and back of the ball, which rests on the target line) and not fanning it open.

After going 2 feet back, your right arm should relax and bend. Your right wrist will also bend into a natural throwing position. Looking down at your right hand, you should not see the inside of the hand. You should see the back of your hand and the first knuckle of your index finger. Next, practice the first half of the takeaway, right hand only, with the left hand next to but not on the club. Again, halfway back you should see some of the back of the hand and the first knuckle on the index finger. The right palm should feel like it's looking back and away from the target. Finally, reach up and add the left hand but continue to feel the right hand pull the club away to a throwing position.

● No. 9

Take the club back inside

Let the clubhead continue through the ball low
along the ground on the line to the target.

— *Gene Littler*

Players who have fallen into the bad habit of taking the club back to the outside, that is, taking the club back by moving the arms out and away from the body, often embrace this advice as a remedy to improving their weak slices. They soon discover, however, that it is a siren's song.

I've also seen players, mostly at the intermediate level, start taking the club back inside when they're contacting the ball at impact with an open clubface, thus causing a slice. The erroneous thought is, "I'm slicing so I must be cutting across the ball from the outside to inside." This is a good guess but unfortunately it is incorrect.

Beginners, I've found, often start with the correct movement—taking the club back along the target line—but then start the club forward with the arms on the downswing. At contact, their arms have come back to the ball with both hands and clubface looking to the right of target. The result is that the ball goes where the hands and clubface are looking—to the right!

To compensate, they then move the club over the top with the arms; that is, they swing the club out as they start the downswing from the top and then in, moving the clubhead across the target line from the far side to the near side closer to the body, on the downswing. Their attempt is logical. To get the ball started, move to the left. This movement creates the side spin at impact, which makes the ball slice. Understand the role of the hands, especially the right hand, which is to deliver the clubhead squarely to the target line and into the back of the ball.

There are really two ways of increasing your distance. You can learn to swing the clubhead faster. Or you can learn to deliver it to the ball more accurately . . .

— Jack Nicklaus

A righteous path

The path of the club in the takeaway travels for a short distance along the target line and then gradually inside the target line. But all of the "around" part of the golf swing comes from the body. The club moves back and up as the body coils. As you move the clubhead back, keep the hands in front of the coiling torso. If you exaggerate your inside takeaway and then try to approach the ball from the inside, you hit blocks and hooks—blocks when the hands are late in squaring the clubface and hooks when the body stops and the hands move past the body, thus shutting the clubface or moving the club's toe ahead of its heel at impact.

Better players tend to develop the problem of routing the club too much from the inside. When this results in hooks they attribute the cause to an overly active right hand. They are sure that the right hand is overrotating the face of the club through the impact area, thus closing the face.

The path of the club in the takeaway travels for a short distance along the target line (1) and then gradually inside the line (2). As you move the clubhead back, keep the hands in front of the coiling torso.

A player's overly rotated right hand can be the culprit, but it's seldom the case. However, the right hand always plays a role in the solution. To hit straighter shots the player must focus on using the right hand to start the club back on line and return it on line with the clubface square at contact. A hook is only created when the release and rotation of the clubhead passes the rotation of the center of the body. The following drill can help ingrain this movement.

Should I take the club back inside or straight back? Low and straight doesn't work because you are standing to the side of the ball. You don't have to worry about the fact that the club moves to the inside. As long as your arms stay "connected" to your body, and you turn, your club will move to the inside. The challenge is getting the club to come up the correct amount as it moves inside. Straight back is off the (swing) plane.

— Hank Haney

THE TAKE ON THE TAKEAWAY

The touring pros put together their advice and lessons in a recently published book, *The PGA Tour Complete Book of Golf*. Their "take" on the takeaway is extremely useful in our discussion of the ill-conceived inside takeaway. The takeaway is the best opportunity for setting the club in motion at a manageable pace. It is also the best chance to get the club started on the proper path. Here the word path refers to the movement of the clubhead throughout the swing. Ideally, the club will travel on the longest possible—or widest—path throughout your swing because the longer the arc of the swing, the more speed it will build up, increasing the distance the ball will travel.

You want the club to remain on a path that will return it to the ball from an angle just inside the target line. (The club does not travel along the target line—a straight line—for very long because you swing the club around your body.) Following this path provides the best chance of the clubhead's being square at impact. To keep the club on this path all the way to impact is a challenge, but it is almost impossible to accomplish if you don't start the club away from the ball on a direct path for the first 2 feet; that is, until your hands are just past your back leg. At this point the wrists will start to bend as the right arm folds at the elbow and the torso coils. If you start your swing by immediately moving the club off that initial straight-back path—either to the inside or the outside—you dramatically reduce your chances of hitting a solid straight shot.

Drill

Here is a drill to help you learn the feeling of the proper takeaway and return. Using a pitching wedge, gripping with the right hand only, hit several balls off a tee. Allow the body to wind up naturally as the right hand goes to a throwing position. Allow the wrist to bend naturally back and the right elbow to fold the arm to achieve a throwing position while the body coils. Then allow the wrist to return the club along the target line as the body uncoils. This will give you the feeling of meeting the ball squarely.

To learn the feeling of proper takeaway and return, use a pitching wedge, gripping with the right hand only. Achieve a throwing position of the right hand and body (1), then move through naturally and allow the right hand and clip the ball off the tee (2).

● No. 10

Make a one-piece takeaway

Moving the club, hands, arms, chest and shoulders away together as a unit will start the clubhead away low and your backswing will be full and wide. Just as it should be.

— *David Leadbetter*

It's hard to argue that a one-piece takeaway, as helpful as it is, might get you into trouble, especially when you see what Tiger Woods has done with it. The first move away from the ball is crucial. It sets in motion a sequence of actions that ultimately lead back to the ball. We want the golf swing to start in unison but we also want the body to move sequentially in the right order. So the one-piece takeaway sounds like a good idea because it gets the entire body moving at once. But does it?

The trouble arises in the one-piece takeaway not when the golfer simultaneously engages the hands, wrists, arms, and shoulders—which are then locked in an inverted isosceles triangle—but when he or she neglects to move the body onto the back leg. When this happens you've got a lot of tension and a swing that is not synchronized and free, but locked and rigid.

Do not make an early break with the hands on the backswing, except when doing a drill. Move everything together—the club, hand, arms, and torso.

Better players actually initiate their swings from the ground up with athletic feel in the feet and legs. Some kick their right knee toward the ball, thus creating a forward press. Others make a small step or slight shift from front to back into the right leg and then start the club in motion. Exclusive focus on taking the club back leads to problems. To avoid them, learn to incorporate the feet and legs as part of the initial movement of the body onto the back leg. Your sense of body rhythm and balance comes through your feet. Stay ready and athletic.

A simple one two motion

We want the clubhead to have freedom of movement, and the rigid or barred arm of a one-piece takeaway can eliminate this freedom. I like players to think

In a one-piece takeaway, better players initiate their swings from the ground up with athletic feel in the feet and legs. Some kick the right knee toward the ball (1) thus creating a forward press. As the body coils, the weight stays inside the right leg (2).

of a simple one-two motion that occurs right after the waggle or pre-takeaway motion; that is, when the club starts moving, the body starts moving to the back leg and coiling. This prevents swaying and moving the bottom of the swing too far toward the right foot. The weight stays inside the right leg as the left knee turns slightly inward. As the club moves back, we want it to remain out in front of the body—opposite the sternum—until it moves up and over the right shoulder. (Do not allow it to fall off course and move immediately behind you. This will "trap" the club behind you and make it difficult to get the face of the club square to the ball on the downswing.)

A good way to phrase this would be, "Move everything together." This allows the player to realize it's not just a one-piece takeaway with the hands and arms, but it's also the movement and coiling of the torso. This helps your timing because the hands don't get too far ahead of the body in the backswing. The body, then, will have enough time to coil before initiating the forward movement in the downswing. Any forced or hurried movements during the golf swing will cause unfavorable results.

Feel the clubhead

Always try to "feel" the clubhead as you swing the club. Don't simply think about hitting the ball. Think about the movement of the club as you swing the clubhead. That way, you'll relieve the tension in your hands and allow your body movements to synchronize with the swing of the clubhead. No matter how many movements you make, your goal is to maintain a sense of connection to the clubhead while swinging it.

> *Those who are able to sense what it means to "swing the clubhead" will find that they can thus cover up a multitude of sins, and those who sense it not will find that no amount of striving for perfection in positioning will quite take its place.*
>
> — *Bobby Jones*

A shake, waggle, or tap

One way to make a one-piece takeaway work for you is to incorporate a little waggle—some kind of preswing movement—at address. We want motion in the clubhead (movement of the hands), feet, or legs, which prepares the body to move. Choose whatever is most comfortable. You can tap the club, or move it slightly back. Some touring pros move the heel of the club to the other side of the target line and then begin the takeaway. Whatever it takes to reduce tension and get you moving is okay. Once the body is moved into first gear—via a tap of the club on the ground, or kicking of the right knee—you're ready to move everything together in the takeaway.

Check your position

Here is a way to check the position on the takeaway. Take the club back with the right hand only to approximately 2 feet, and then place the left hand on the grip. This should be the position you would move to in a one-piece takeaway. The club should still be opposite your sternum. Beyond this the club moves up and back as the body coils. Another technique is to put the grip end of the club on your belt buckle and move the clubhead back and away from the ball to approximately 2 feet. This keeps the club centered on your torso until you're ready to move the club up over your shoulder as you complete the coiling of the torso.

Put the grip end of the club on your belt buckle and move the clubhead back approximately 2 feet. This keeps the club centered on your torso.

When I settle into my shot, I give a slight shake, rattle and roll. My hips are a big part of my swing—both the angle of the tilt from them and their alignment with the target. When I get set, I feel a little flex in my knees, and then I just try to slide the club away from the ball very slowly. I would say almost everyone out (on the PGA Tour) here does it the same before every shot, and that it's a good idea for the everyday player to use the same routine every time as well.

— Ernie Els

● No. 11

Turn your shoulders

A great many players turn their shoulders and think that their hip action is correct. What they don't realize is that you can turn the shoulders while keeping the hips fixed, but when you turn the hips, the shoulders go along.

— Tommy Armour

The phrase I prefer to "turn your shoulders" is "coil your torso."

Coil it into your back leg. When you do this the shoulders turn in response to the hands and arms taking the club back. As you coil, feel how the takeaway with the hands and arms stretches the muscles in the left side of the body. Additionally, the hands can now sense and feel what the clubhead is doing in motion and where it's looking in relation to your intended target.

Here is an important key: coil your abdomen and entire midsection area into your back leg. Properly executed, the sternum should face away from the target. Your base, that is, the lower body, should be stable and under control with the weight distributed inside the feet.

Flexibility, body structure, and posture significantly influence the amount of body rotation and coil, but stretch as far as possible without losing balance. Don't overstretch. If you do, you'll lose your foundation (balance and stability) and you'll weaken your swing. The purpose of coiling is to stretch the muscles through the abdomen and across the lower back—especially the latissimus dorsi muscles that flank each side of the lower and middle back. This builds energy for unleashing the downswing.

To continue your coil and stretch the body, brace your right leg. This will do several helpful things. It will allow your torso to wind or coil more easily. It will prevent swaying. It will generate power by building resistance between the upper body and lower body. And it will secure the weight onto your back foot. A braced right leg, slightly flexed, is another key to a solid and sufficiently coiled position at the top.

Correct spine angle is 90 degrees to clubshaft

Let's briefly look at what constitutes a good coil. The upper spine must be as straight as possible—for every degree that your spine rounds from the bottom of the shoulder blades to the back of the neck you lose 1½ degrees of rotation. The spine at address needs to be set up at an angle that is 90 degrees or perpendicular to the shaft of the club. The rotation of the shoulders also needs to be 90 degrees or perpendicular to the spine during the backswing and through the swing. The lower body must remain stable and support coiling of the torso and the rotation of the shoulders.

Watch out for these problems

Several problems occur with golfers who focus on shoulder turn. The first is that the club takes off way to the inside instead of directly away from the ball.

The second is that players don't know how much to turn. They've heard that a big turn will yield power, so they turn too much. The result is that the lower body breaks down and loses balance. Lastly they forget that the body has to drive onto the front leg and unwind through the ball. When examined on videotape, an overturn in the backswing has the club slowing down, not accelerating, at impact. The acceleration of the hands, arms, and clubhead must come from an athletic movement from the lower body driving and unwinding around the inside of the front leg.

When you concentrate solely on turning your shoulders in the backswing, the tendency is to

The lower body must remain stable and support coiling of the torso and the rotation of the shoulders.

SAY WHAT YOU MEAN, MEAN WHAT YOU SAY

The premise of this book is that words are powerful. They can lead you to the Promised Land, or down the road of good intentions. The word *turn*, I fear, is such a word.

Turn is a tension-free, passive word. It conjures up images of a gate swinging lazily and easily on its hinges, a hand and wrist arching 30 degrees left or right of the elbow joint. It does not suggest stored energy, or explosive movement upon return to its original position. Turn can also suggest the moving of a singular part of the body, in this case the shoulders, rotating independently of other parts of the body. In describing the required body movement of the backswing, it fails to capture the true essence of the movement. In short, it is a poor word to crystallize the movement required in the backswing.

That's why I prefer *coil*. As in "coil like a spring." This suggests a stretching of the large muscles of the back, which is the desired action. Like a spring, golfers coil the torso, store energy, and thus increase the torque necessary for generating power and speed of the hands in the downswing and through impact. The hands on a clock—yes, they turn. But a spring? It coils and uncoils.

So, with the shoulders, don't turn them. Coil the torso. Coil and unwind.

---

move your arms and hands much too far behind you. Then, the only way to get back to the point of contact is for the arms to move out and away from the body. This brings the club outside and then across the target line—known as "coming over the top." The results are not good: either a pull or a slice.

When shoulders overrotate, you have no chance

The next move (from the top) is to slide the weight onto the front side and unwind the upper body, bringing the arms and hands down alongside the body and firing the clubhead through the hitting zone.

The entire right side of your body—but especially the legs and torso—controls the amount of turn that takes place in the swing. It provides a certain amount of resistance that slows the rotation of your knees, hips, and shoulders. When you concentrate solely on "turning the shoulders," you risk

Place your right hand on your stomach and coil into the inside of the back leg. Feel the muscle tension in the right thigh as the leg stabilizes.

neglecting some of the other movements of the body. This can put the swing out of synchronization. For example, when the shoulders move independently you can find yourself having "overrotated" at the top.

Drills

1. Place right hand on your stomach and coil into the inside of the back leg. Feel the muscle tension in the right thigh and groin as the leg stabilizes. Feel the muscles across the back and up the left side stretch

fully. Next, move into the front foot and leg, unwinding fully to a balanced finish on the left or front leg.

2. Practice the first part of the takeaway with your eyes closed. As the hands and arms start the club away, feel the center of your body move with your hands and into the right leg. Repeat several times until you can feel the coordination of the two motions.

● **No. 12**

Move your left knee behind the ball (in the backswing)

Many shots are spoiled at the last instant by efforts to add a few more yards. This impedes, rather than aids the stroke.

— Bobby Jones

Bobby Jones could easily have been talking about moving the left knee (along with the entire body) further back, behind the ball in the takeaway and backswing. To do this would be a case of "subtraction by addition." The added backswing would produce a less reliable and less powerful shot. The fact is, in the backswing you should not be focusing on the moving of your knees. The knees should be responding to the other parts of the body that are moving.

For example, the natural response of the knee is to move toward the ball, out and away from the body, as the torso coils in the backswing. If there is too much backward motion of the left knee, then the right leg will respond

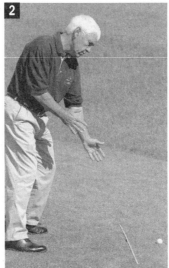

In the backswing the natural response of the knees is to move toward the ball, out and away from the body, as the torso coils. Think of your knees as moving in a "pumping action," rather than sliding backward.

by breaking down; that is, it will allow your weight to roll onto the outside of the right leg. Balance is lost and the bottom of your swing arc moves closer to the right foot. One result is that your swing will bottom out behind the ball rather than just in front of it. Instead, think of your knees as moving more in a "pumping action," rather than sliding backward. This should prevent excessive weight shift.

The intent of this tip is to get the weight moving onto the right side in the backswing. Keep in mind that you can get into trouble if you move the left knee too far to the rear (laterally). The worst case is moving the left knee so far to the rear that you create a reverse pivot. Just remember this: do not move the left knee so far that it shifts behind the ball. A position that is opposite the ball is about as far as the knee can move before you lose balance. What about the right knee? In the backswing the right leg should maintain a slight flex at the knee. You should not lock the right knee or straighten the leg. When the left knee moves too much laterally it creates a locking or bowing of the right knee. Neither allows you to coil the torso and load the weight into the inside of the right leg. Also, it's more important to know what the clubhead is doing than what your left and right knees are doing.

Drill

Stand with your arms and hands extended straight in front, hands slightly apart, legs flexed slightly. Pull the right hand toward your body while simultaneously pumping the left hand away from the body, as if you were punching a ball teed waist high. Notice how the left knee works outward, not back. On the through swing, as you punch with your right hand, the right knee moves slightly outward. Get the feel of the pumping action of the legs. They do not slide laterally, and the left knee never moves behind the ball.

● No. 13

Keep your weight inside the right leg in the backswing

Retain the flex that you created in the right knee at address all the way to the top of your backswing. Any sensation of pressure in your right knee and thigh is a positive sign that you have offset any tendency to bow that knee outward.

— David Leadbetter

The problem with this advice—which is valid—is not that players habitually misinterpret its meaning. Rather, it's a case of getting the "cart before the horse." We do want to keep the weight within the stance on the backswing. But when

Place your left hand on your sternum and coil into your rear leg and hips. Push off and uncoil the torso inside the front foot and leg; avoid rolling the weight onto the outside of the front leg.

it comes to the backswing we need always to look first at the width of the stance and the flex in the legs and then to check for proper weight movement.

Here are the key steps to take to avoid weight shift problems. Place your feet properly, that is, so that the inside of your back foot is aligned outside your back hip with the weight centered on both feet. Tilt first from the hips and then relax your knees. It is essential in the address and setup that you position the inside of the right foot outside the right hip. Once you are properly set up and aligned, focus on coiling into the inside of the back leg. Concentrate on stabilizing the body during the coil so that the downswing transition is seamless and powerful. And remember that the head has to be allowed to move with the body as it coils into the back leg and moves up and out of the shot after impact.

Unfortunately, a lot of players start the swing by pushing away with the left arm (as part of the one-piece takeaway). With a stance that is too narrow it is easy to push the weight too far to the right onto the outside of the right leg. The result is loss of balance, an unstable base. This is also encountered when your stance has too much flex in the legs and no leaning or bending from the hips. You can also lose stability in the right leg if there is too much turning in the backswing.

We want the right leg to be the rock-solid base of the backswing. It is the key to building a powerful swing. But if it is moving around or flexing to the rear at the knee, it cannot function as a base. It simply cannot support the correct movement, that of coiling inside the right leg and inside the right hip.

Drill

Place your hands on your stomach and coil into your rear leg and hip. Notice how the leg stays stable to support this movement. Now practice changing direction by going forward, pushing off the inside of the right foot. When pushing off to go forward, uncoil the torso inside the front foot and leg and avoid rolling the weight onto the outside of the front leg.

No. 14

Swing the club to parallel at the top of the backswing

Whatever amount of controlled turn you can make while feeling as if you have something in reserve is the right length of backswing for you.

— Butch Harmon

This idea depends on the flexibility of the player. It's true that for some players the backswing is completed when the club is parallel to the target line. Players who are extraordinarily flexible can go beyond parallel. Others—

Move your right hand into a throwing position. Next, reach with your left hand and place it on the grip. If your left hand comfortably reaches your right hand, you've found the preferred "at-the-top" position.

such as PGA Tour player Craig Stadler—have less flexibility and will not get the club to parallel.

The purpose of the backswing is coil the torso and get the body into a strong position to launch the forward swing. Getting the club to parallel may not necessarily accomplis this. Sometimes in focusing on getting to the top you create an independent hands and arms movement that lacks a good coil into the back leg.

Remember, it's your individual flexibility that determines the length of your backswing. Everyone's "top" is not the same. PGA Senior tour players Dana Quigley and Alan Doyle keep their respective "tops" below shoulder height but still create tremendous coil and clubhead speed. If you try to reach too far back and up, as in following the advice, "reach for the sky," you loosen your base, create too long of a swing and dissipate all your clubhead speed before impact.

TO EACH HIS OWN SWING

PGA teacher T. J. Tomasi, Ph.D. is a proponent of the idea that golf-swing mechanics vary with golfers' body types. According to Tomasi, one type, what Tomasi terms the "Width Player," a golfer with a muscular, broad-chested build as exemplified by PGA players Jim Albus and Craig Stadler, need not swing the club parallel in the backswing. In fact, the preferred "at the top" position for this type of player is what Tomasi calls a "low hands, high clubhead" position. He advises this player to take the hands to shoulder height but not to "reach for the sky" a la Jack Nicklaus or John Daly, which brings the clubshaft to parallel and past it. According to Tomasi, "You (the burly, stocky player) can't afford "high hands, high clubhead" because your flexibility won't allow you to reach up that high." He adds, "Remember, you're strong enough to swing short—that is why we call it muscular advantage. It's your muscles that allow you the most direct power route to the ball." For all of us—but especially the ex-fullbacks and linebackers among us—it's something to think about!

Drill

Assume a right-hand throwing position. Take your hand and raise it as if you were going to throw a baseball. Next, reach with your left hand and clasp your right hand. If you cannot reach your right hand with your left hand and arm while stretching your left side and maintaining your base, then bring your right hand to a three-quarter position. Again, stretch your left side and see if you can comfortably reach your right hand. If you can't, take the right hand to one-half throwing position. Your ideal backswing would have the right hand and arm in a throwing position with the left side fully stretched and your base solid and balanced.

III BACKSWING AND FORWARD SWING

● **No. 15**

Keep your head still

Although my head swivels to the right as I start back, the back of my neck stays in the same place throughout the backswing. This is the fulcrum or pivotal point or hub of my swing.

— *Jack Nicklaus*

You should avoid excessive movement of the head. However, here's a much better verbal image to get across the right idea: "Keep the head quiet." The word "still" implies stationary, not moving at all. It suggests rigidity. It brings on tension.

Try to allow for some head movement while maintaining balance. Think of keeping the head "quiet," but not totally still. Quiet means that you can move the head perceptibly back, down, or forward when coiling and uncoiling around the spine as long as you maintain balance. Quiet also means allowing natural head movement forward as the body moves into and around the front leg to a full finish on the forward swing.

Let's look at this logically. Your head is attached to your body and your body is centered between your feet and legs. The base of your backswing is the inside of the right hip and thigh, and the

Keep your head quiet, not still. Quiet means that you can move the head perceptibly back (2) when coiling and forward (4) when uncoiling.

base of the forward swing is the inside of the left hip and thigh. The body must move to the back leg in the backswing and onto and around the front leg on the forward swing. You must allow the head to move naturally back with the body and naturally forward with the body to a natural, balanced finish on the left leg.

Everyone moves the head slightly

All good players move their head slightly in the swing. If the body is not allowed some natural movement in the backswing, you get a reverse pivot. This is when the weight remains on the left side during the backswing and then is transferred to the right side on the downswing, or exactly opposite of the correct technique. It is caused primarily by players trying to keep the head still.

Thus, it is natural on the backswing for the body to move into the back leg and for the head to come along with it. And it is natural for the head to move slightly downward in the downswing and forward through impact in the forward swing. The eyes naturally look up to follow the flight of the ball after it leaves the clubface. However, it is not natural, nor desirable, for the head to move toward (closer) or away from the target line during any part of the swing. This is a sign that your balance is unstable, usually from overworking the arms, or from rocking the weight onto your heels in the backswing and then onto the toes on the forward swing. The result can be shots struck off the toe, heel, or hosel (the dreaded shank) of the club.

The supposition that the eyes must remain fixed throughout the follow-through on the spot from which the ball was hit is completely erroneous. This is unnatural and retards the free and full turn of the shoulders.

— Byron Nelson

Why do players try to keep the head still?

Players try to keep the head still for two reasons. First, they mistakenly think absolutely no movement of the head is the correct technique. Somewhere, at some time, they've heard this, or think they've read this, and they try to follow it. Second, they believe if they keep their head riveted on the ball they will improve contact. For solid contact, keep the swing rotation inside the base of your stance and maintain balance throughout the swing. When you try to restrict the movement of the head in the backswing, it goes too far backward in the downswing and at impact. You find the ball with the club-head through your hands as your body moves athletically in balance. Make no attempt to stay behind the ball, move naturally (as if throwing a ball) to a well-balanced relaxed finish, fully on the front leg.

Keep the body rotating into and around the insides of the legs, which stay in place during the swing. Solid contact is a result of good balance throughout the swing. As the body moves naturally through the sequence of swing motions, the hands find the ball with the clubhead.

SWING LIKE PAUL BUNYAN

Beginning golfers often restrict their swings in an effort to make contact with the ball. It's understandable. After all, it is intimidating to have such a long-shafted club with a very small striking area trying to contact a very small ball. It's not an easy task to contemplate.

I've always thought it would be useful to give a beginner an ax, bring him alongside a tree, and ask him to strike the tree. So many of the dynamics would change. First, you wouldn't hold the ax like you're holding a bird. When you'd swing, you would not just try to hit the tree but you would try to bury the ax into the tree.

You would not restrict your swing because you have no fear of missing the tree, and you wouldn't get any negative feedback—slice, hook, or topped ball. You'd have no fear of mishitting and you'd have a natural swinging motion that would not be restricted by a head held much too still. Believe me, if you want to learn to hit a golf ball properly, try swinging like Paul Bunyan.

Role of the eyes

The eyes play a much smaller role in hitting the golf ball than you realize. You can hit a ball blindfolded by using kinesthetic feel, that is, the body's autonomically sensing and directing its movement. The mind's eye sees the ball and the body sends the clubhead along the path that strikes the ball. Try it—you'll make solid contact and send the ball flying.

The eyes should release naturally after contact. This allows the body to continue a free rotation and helps the clubhead stay lower to the ground through and past impact. Here is a simple exercise for training the eyes to respond to the flight of the ball. Using a sand or pitching wedge, hit teed balls to a target at 50 yards. Immediately after contact roll your head and eyes up, catching sight of the ball. Follow the ball as you rotate out of the shot.

No one pays enough attention to just how much we play by sound. Try to make even beginners aware of it, how important it is to listen and feel. Try to hit the ball squarely, listen, and then try to reproduce that sound. The more you hear it, the better you're going to swing it.

— Gloria Armstrong

● No. 16

Keep your head down

I never did see the sense in keeping my head down. The only reason I play golf is to see where the ball goes.

— Charles Price

"You peeked."

Have you heard this friendly assessment from your playing partner right after you've topped a ball and grounded it down the fairway? Most of us have, but it isn't so. I've seen thousands of golf swings and I have yet to see someone look up before hitting the ball. It's a mirage. It just doesn't happen.

Unfortunately, a catastrophic remedy then follows bad analysis—the player adjusts by rededicating himself to keeping his head down. This leads to restricted coiling and uncoiling. For one thing, when you lower the head, literally drop it down between hunched shoulders, you ruin the spine angle. The upper spine rounds off because the head is buried in the shoulders, and for every degree you diminish this spine angle you lose 1-12 degrees in body rotation.

What is the correct action? Get the head up so that the spine angle remains straight, not rounded.

I know that when players keep the head down they are trying to keep their eyes on the ball; they're trying to make good contact. But the eyes are not the most critical component of finding and hitting the golf ball. Just looking at the ball does not guarantee that you will hit it solidly each time. The head that needs attention is the head on the end of the clubshaft. It needs to be moved away and then into the ball squarely. And your hands and arms and body need the space under your head, or chin, to help the club do so.

THE MONEY COIL

T. J. Tomasi, Ph.D., director of the Players School, describes the head movement for what he identifies as the Width Player, that is, the short, stocky, barrel-chested player personified by PGA Tour player Craig Stadler: "The upper spine floats behind the ball as the backswing coil develops. The chest turns away from the target, taking everything in the upper body with it, including the head. The head stays positioned in the middle of the shoulders as the body turns back and through. We call the head/spine float the moving coil. Students invariably say it feels like a sway, but it isn't. A sway occurs when the right hip moves laterally outside the right heel, whereas in the moving coil the spine and head float back as the weight moves to the right hip, not outside it. This is a necessary accommodation to a body type not suited to twisting itself up like a pretzel."

At address keep the head up so that the spine angle remains straight not rounded. A lowered head leads to a restricted coiling and uncoiling.

Taking the proper stance and head position

Here's how to take the proper stance and correctly position the head. Tilt forward first from the hips and keep your spine angle throughout. Don't drop your head. Look down with your eyes to see the ball. Place a ball on a tee, close your eyes, and swing. Feel the rhythm and balance. Visualize the clubhead moving away and then down and into the back of the ball. Open your eyes and continue with half-swings, brushing the grass.

Next, take a full swing and hit the ball. Focus on making the clubhead brush the grass after impact. With the proper spine angle and without your head so low that it impedes the body's rotation, your right side will move freely through the ball, enabling you to hit the ball solidly. The very nature of extension through and past the ball must come from the right hand and right side of the body.

After contact let your eyes naturally follow the flight of the ball (1) and move the body to a well-balanced finish (2).

Head-lifting is caused by fear and anxiety. You are seeking the result before you have struck the ball. You did not trust your swing.

— *Ernest Jones*

Eyes release naturally immediately after contact

When does the head come up? Jack Nicklaus believes that "the trick is to let the head swivel and rise only when the natural momentum of the through-swing forces it to do so." I would tell you to attempt to watch the contact but let your eyes naturally follow the flight of the ball and move the entire body to a well-balanced finish.

The top of the spine, on which the head rests, must remain stable throughout the swing. Any shifting, such as too much sideways, up, or down—including lowering the head—diminishes the effectiveness of the body's coiling and uncoiling action. This not only shuts down power but causes balls to be topped or missed altogether.

Take the emphasis off the head and let the body coil naturally into the back leg on the backswing. Unwind around the front leg to a well-balanced finish with the weight fully on the front foot and leg.

To those of you who say that you feel your head come up through impact, please understand why. As you overuse your arms on the downswing without using your body, your arms move into your body too much. The mind senses this and raises the spine so you don't slam the club into the ground. What is the correct alternative to this feeling of the body moving up? Let the body move through the ball. Contact with the golf ball is with or through the right hand. The right hand ultimately delivers the clubhead into the ball.

As Henry Cotton said, your right hand is the "finder" hand, not the eyes.

● No. 17

You can't swing too slowly

> *There is a blood relationship between waggle and tempo. Show me someone who has quick, short waggle and I will show you someone who has a quick, short swing. Show me a long, languid waggle, and I'll show you person who has got a long, flowing swing.*
>
> *— Roger Maltbie*

The truth of the matter is that you can swing too slow and too fast.

Although "you can't swing too slow" might be good advice for players who apply too much arm speed, it gives the golfer very little direction in how to interpret what is too slow. The terms slow and fast are hard to define.

Every golfer is different. For example, Jack Nicklaus' swings slower than Arnold Palmer, but neither swings too slow or too fast.

What's slow for you may not be slow for me. I prefer that we get away from using the term slow and that you think about swinging "softly" or "gently." This will give you a little better idea—an image for the mind's eye to focus on and translate into action should you apply the advice to your swing.

You can't place too much emphasis on smoothness in your swing, but you can overdo the slowness. Many golfers—probably the majority—swing too fast, destroying their rhythm and any chance they might have of timing their swing properly. But many players do swing too slowly. A slow, deliberate swing increases the prospect of creating tension, and it certainly prohibits free motion. Moreover, a painfully deliberate backswing often causes, as a reaction, an extremely fast downswing, and this means the sure ruination of good rhythm.

— Byron Nelson

Rate your swing speed

One way to get at the correct swing speed is to give your swing a rating. For example, say you rate your normal swing speed at a speed of 30 mph. Try taking a swing (without the ball) while moving the club at what you feel is 10 mph. Keep the speed constant throughout. Now drop it down to 5 mph, and then go up to 15 or 20 mph. Through experimentation, you can develop a sense of the different swing speeds and what produces better results. You may even find you want to gauge your speed depending on your club selection.

Now let's add the ball and continue our exercise. The objective is to move the clubhead freely at one of your geared-down rates, say 10 or 15 mph, but not at a slow enough speed to bring on tension, interrupt the rhythm, or lose clubhead speed at impact. This exercise demonstrates that you can achieve

A powerful swing is rhythmic. Anytime you look to create more power by swinging harder, tension adversely affects your swing. Not only will you distort your rhythm and tempo, but you'll also diminish clubhead speed, thus reducing the length of your shots.

solid contact at any speed of swing, that solid contact is achieved through a paced, rhythmic swing, and that this is the key to unlocking power. Take a club (say a 7 iron) back to shoulder height or just below and then start the downswing. Swing at a pace you visualize as your normal speed, which you've gauged at 30 mph. Repeat at 20 mph, then 10 mph. Now go back to 30 mph and move to 40 mph, all the time keeping a constant pace (rhythm) and concentrating on striking the ball in the center of the club, square to the target line. The ball will literally jump off the clubface because you are transferring so much of the generated energy to the ball. Then take the club back to slightly higher than shoulder height and repeat.

You're learning to hit the ball softly and rhythmically but with authority, and you're not slowing down your swing to do it.

Speed of swing versus control and accuracy

Any time you look to create more power by swinging harder, you're in danger of losing accuracy and control. In the game of baseball, the long, hard swings generated by home run sluggers produce more mishits than the shorter, more controlled swings of the "table setters" (players who slash singles and doubles by making solid contact on each pitch). Sluggers don't hit the ball on the fat part—or sweet spot—of the bat as often. The same is true in golf. Swing the club too hard and you will contact the ball "fat" or "thin" or on the perimeter of the clubface. Result? Errant, inconsistent shots.

Also, by trying to create additional power with your hands, wrists, and shoulders, you will create tension, which reduces—not increases—clubhead speed. And you need clubhead speed if you are to generate power and distance. Jack Nicklaus got his hands around this issue with this thought: "There are really two ways of increasing your distance. You can learn to swing the clubhead faster. Or you can learn to deliver it to the ball more consistently."

Softer, gentler means consistency

When you make a swing using the image of softer or gentler you will make solid contact more consistently. If we can achieve this, it will breed confidence in the results of swinging the club at an even pace and not surging in the downswing to generate distance. Rhythm, timing, and contact at the center of the clubface . . . these produce consistency of distance.

Consistent distance is one of my teaching goals, especially with better players. Improvement comes when a player can produce a better pattern or cluster of shots at the same distance. I want the dispersion between long and short to be minimal. For example, if a player hits a 9-iron 140 yards, we want the ball to fly 137 to 143 yards each time. To do this, the player has to tap into his optimum swing speed and swing at that speed every time. Remember, swinging too fast or too slow won't get you there.

No. 18

Swing easy, hit it hard

You can't take a car from a dead start and put it immediately up to 70 miles per hour. No matter how powerful your engine, you must have a gradual acceleration of speed. So it is in a golf swing.

— Mickey Wright

These words make sense in theory, but try executing this command. The brain is stymied with the thought, "What does this really mean?" A simple explanation states that the golfer needs to be relaxed to hit the ball with maximum authority. A tension-free, fluid swing allows for optimum clubhead speed and consistent ballstriking.

I've seen many golfers struggle with this concept when trying to execute their individual interpretation. The common mistake is that players focus on the arms instead of the clubhead. They swing them too slowly going away from the ball and then they whip them through the hitting areas, creating a wide variety of mishits. If you could read a computer printout of their thought process it would say, "Start easy, now put the pedal to the metal."

Effortless power versus powerful effort

If applying extra force with your arms and hands in an attempt to accelerate the club before impact produces erratic shots in both distance and direction, then what generates clubhead speed? For one, the body must lead the start of the downswing. When you move the body ahead of the club it gains speed without any concentrated, extra effort from the arms. Centrifugal force propels the clubhead, which is positioned farthest from your body and thus receives all the energy and gains speed. My advice toward developing a sound golf swing is to put forth effortless power rather than a powerful effort. Learn to relax and let your body unwind around your front leg. Allow your hands to react so they can bring the clubhead squarely to the ball as you are continuing through the hitting area.

The muscles have to be relaxed to stretch and act with quickness. "Swing easy" connotes a lack of muscular tension. It also connotes a free movement of the club. The club has to move unencumbered through the hitting area. You don't want to feel yourself actually steering the ball in a direction. Some players actually lock their arms in trying to control the clubhead, and this makes it impossible to hit the ball hard.

Stay balanced, avoid overswinging

A controlled swing allows the entire body to work in unison. Overswinging disrupts timing and balance—the arms are controlling the motion. With better players the legs and hips fire too aggressively and the hands fall too far behind the lower body. The club is trapped behind the rear hip with no clear path to the ball. The brain then sends a message to the hands that they need to hurry to get to the ball. The body will stop rotating and respond by flipping the clubhead around the ball. As a result the ball will be hooked or the player will start responding by blocking shots to the right.

A similar problem occurs when the body does not move into the front foot and leg, and the arms lead the downswing sequence. The arms have two paths to the ball: (1) into or close alongside the body, or (2) out around the body (this is called coming "over the top"). What we want is the hands maintaining their relationship to the body. This would bring the clubhead on a path best described as "in (alongside the body) to square (down the target line) to in (follow through)." Otherwise, shots will be pulled or hooked to the left, or sliced to the right.

> *I think the everyday golfer has a tendency to confuse the word aggressive with the notion of killing the ball or swinging as hard as he can. When you hear these guys on the tour talking about making an aggressive swing, that's not what they mean. Making an aggressive swing is concentrating on making a full swing and not quitting on it or trying to steer it. Aggressive means just making a good full confident swing without backing off.*
>
> *— Mark O'Meara*

Focus on tempo and timing

The key is to think tempo. If you maintain a good tempo, your body movements remain fluid. Quieting everything down fosters good tempo and helps the body make a natural movement into and around the front foot and leg. The unwinding of the body allows the hands to then fire through on contact freely and fully, releasing the clubhead. When the body smoothly leads the downswing the hands naturally lag and as the body unwinds the hands release through the hitting area.

To gain a visual image of a player who swings easy and hits the ball about as hard as anyone, watch the "Big Easy," South African Ernie Els, with a club in his hands. Els appears to have one of the most effortless swings on the PGA tour, but he generates exceptional clubhead speed. His club acceleration can be difficult to detect because his entire body is so smooth in its transition to the ball. There are no bursting, shoving, thrusting, or hurried movements from start to finish. Just a relaxed, powerful swing.

To learn proper tempo and to get a feel for a swing with tempo, practice half swings and focus on center-of-the club contact. Release the eyes to follow the flight of the ball and keep looking down target to the finish.

Drill

To get a feel for a swing with tempo, take half-swings and emphasize center-of-the-club contact with the ball. Take the swing with an easy, fluid motion, not a power surge. Focus on staying relaxed and making solid center-face contact with a free-swinging clubhead. Sometimes players need to begin this drill with short chip shots. This will give you a better feeling of two important parts of the swing sequence: (1) moving or uncoiling onto and around the foot and leg on the forward swing, and (2) allowing the hands to catch up as the body leads the swing.

● No. 19

Move the club along the same path on the forward swing as taken on the backswing

As the club reaches a position horizontal with the ground (at the top), an extension from the butt end (when viewed from overhead and behind along the plane created by the target line and the horizontal clubshaft) should point through the ball and extend toward the target. If it stays in plane it will point back along that same line well into the follow-through. Remember, the clubhead will always follow the butt end.

— Gary Wiren

Discussions of swing planes can be confusing because they're multiple—a backswing plane and a downswing plane. But only one really counts—the plane created as the clubhead is dropped from shoulder height during the downswing and propelled through the impact area. If you stop and think about how the swing is accomplished, you would reject the idea of a single swing plane out of hand. The plane that the club follows on the backswing is not identical to the plane the club follows on the downswing. It's impossible.

However, I like players to sense that the clubhead is returning down the same path when returning to the ball as when it went away.

The correct movement of the body in the downswing naturally narrows and steepens the downswing path. The movement of the body forward into the front foot and leg pulls the arms into the body, thus narrowing the downswing path. The right hand must work in the downswing to force the clubhead back on a direct path to the ball and get the face of the clubhead back looking at the ball prior to impact.

Players should sense that the clubhead is returning down the same path when returning to the ball (2) as when it went away (1).

The most important part of the swing plane involves the clubhead and clubface 2 feet away from the ball and the last 2 feet returning prior to impact. Get the clubface looking at the ball going away and involve the right hand to get it looking at the ball early on the return.

There is no such thing as an absolute and standard plane for all golfers. The correct angle for each person's plane depends on how he is built. A fellow whose legs are proportionately shorter than his arms, for example, necessarily creates a shallow angle for his plane. At the other extreme, a man whose legs are proportionately longer than his arms sets up a very steep angle for himself. Neither plane is incorrect.

— Ben Hogan

Drill

Take the club back to where the shaft parallels the ground. At this point the shaft should be parallel to the target line and the leading edge of the club should face more toward the ball. At halfway back and halfway through, an extension of the clubshaft should point into an extension of the target line. Hit one-half shots off a tee with the feel of the clubshaft half-way back to halfway through. Pay special attention on these half swings to the two-foot area that is back of the point of impact. When moving into and through this area, get the right palm to face toward the ball and your intended target.

● No. 20

Shift your weight

When starting the downswing, my first move is the beginning of transfer of weight back from my right to my left side. I am conscious of pulling the club down with the left hip and shoulder.

— Byron Nelson

Too much emphasis on the idea of shifting leads to problems. As you keep your head still and shift your weight, you create a sway (a lateral movement of the hips outside the feet and legs). Weight does transfer and move with good players in their swings, but the word shift leads to wrong connotations. As the center of the body coils into the back leg, the weight moves to the right. As the body drives into the front foot and leg, the weight moves forward. Trying to shift your weight won't create the proper coiling, driving, and unwinding action of the body. Conversely, the proper coiling action into the back leg and into and around the front leg moves the weight correctly. There's no room here for "swinging and swaying," unless you're headed for the ballroom.

A variety of functions

The legs not only are a source power, they also provide stability and balance. The real power comes from providing a stable base and resistance that enables you to coil and uncoil the torso. The legs facilitate the powerful rotation of the trunk, which results in accelerating the arms and hands, which then fire the clubhead through the impact area.

> *A golf swing can work, after a fashion, even if the center is moved forward towards the hole during the downswing. But moving the center (which in effect means the entire body) during the forward swing reduces any player's ability to generate the greatest possible clubhead speed into impact. In the swings of top professionals . . . as the hips move forward, with the hub or center (middle of the chest, just below the shoulders) held still, the player's head may move slightly back and downward.*
>
> *— Mike Hebron*

When you focus on the idea of shifting your weight, problems can arise. You can shift laterally outside your back leg on the backswing. This results in a variety of mishits—fat, thin, pulled, pushed, or sliced. With this error it's unlikely you'll hit many solid shots.

The legs not only are a source of power, they also provide stability and balance. The power comes from providing a stable base and resistance that enables you to coil (1), to drive into the front foot and leg (2), and uncoil around the front foot and leg as the right hand fully delivers the club (3, 4).

MORE THAN ONE WAY TO SKIN A CAT

When Duffy Waldorf, a top PGA Tour player, wants to troubleshoot the movement of his weight, he focuses on where his weight is when he finishes the swing. He says that turning his shoulders triggers a correct weight shift: "At the start of the swing, I don't really think about how much weight I need to move. I think about turning my shoulders. If I make a good shoulder turn (in the takeaway), my hips also turn as my weight shifts to my back foot. If, in the follow-through, my weight finishes on my front foot, I know I got it shifted correctly in the first place (going back). When I finish with weight still on my back foot, I know my turn isn't right. I know I didn't get it back enough to begin with. So I use where the weight is at my finish to tell me where my weight was during the swing."

Works for Duffy. It may work for you.

When you overshift the hips in the downswing, the legs get out in front of the body. As the body loses support, it loses rotation. The hands, arms, and club get caught behind the body, causing fat shots, blocks, and flip-over hooks.

To start the downswing correctly you must allow the body to move forward into the front leg. Once you have reestablished weight into the front foot and leg the body unwinds to a full finish on top of the front leg. The shift—or gliding—forward starts the downswing. Do not fire the legs or slam the hips foward. Rather, drive your body smoothly into the front foot and leg, maintaining balance and control throughout the move. At impact your left leg must be firm enough to stabilize the unwinding of your trunk and to support the release of the clubhead.

Drill

This is a drill for learning change of direction, what I called the pump drill.

Take the club back to three-quarters and stop. Your weight should be primarily on the inside of your right foot and leg. Now, leading the way with your back and keeping your hands and arms at the top, start forward by moving into your left leg until you feel the weight get onto the inside of the foot and leg. Now, go back up and start down again, letting your hands and arms follow naturally. You should feel that the change of direction is started by the body, not the arms and hands. This builds tempo and improves timing.

No. 21
Pause at the top

There is some psychological mystery about the rushing at the top of the swing I've never been able to solve. The ball is going to stay where it is until it is hit, so there's no valid reason for making a mad dash at it.

— Tommy Armour

I understand why this has been useful for some players. But problems arise when a player exhibits what is called "the urge to surge." Many players tend to increase speed in the change of direction, that is, when they move from the backswing to the forward swing. There is no need to change speed when approaching and leaving "the top." The tempo is constant.

Other players get into trouble with this swing thought because they think that everything—the shoulders, trunk, hips, knees—must stop completely, which is not the case in the so-called pause. When this happens, a player freezes at the top and destroys whatever rhythm he had. The "urge to surge" takes over and the player rushes his downswing.

Don't bring your hands and arms to a dead stop. Keep them moving slowly at the top (1, 2) through the change of direction (3). Allow the body to smoothly change direction and the hands begin their drop into the slot alongside the right leg.

Some teachers insist that this advice gives the player a chance to change the direction in which the club is moving, thus conforming to the law of physics that says any object moving in one direction must come to a complete stop before moving in the opposite direction. The club does stop, but we don't have to think about it. What happens at the top of the swing is that while the club stops for a fraction of a second before changing direction, the center of the body is moving, already starting the downswing. This movement starts before the club comes to a stop.

Many of you are familiar with the swings of Nancy Lopez and Bob Murphy, which display distinct pauses at the top. The question is, are their pauses "dead stops," where everything comes to a distinct halt, or are they idling one part of the body and subtly moving another? I think it's the latter because their hips and knees are moving ever so slightly while the club resets for the downswing. Next time you see them swing, watch their lower body and you'll see that the pause is only with the clubhead.

Lopez and Murphy have slow backswings, which they settle before starting to move forward. But when they restart they move their bodies first, not the arms and hands. With this kind of pause, they exaggerate the quietness or slowness of the hands in the change of direction.

You may be able to use this advice

If this advice causes you to stop the fluidity and rhythm of your swing, then it's not a good swing thought. However, if it can keep your arms from hurrying during the change of direction—but not come to a dead stop—then it's doing some good. When this idea destroys the proper sequence of movements it's really not a good idea. But if it can keep you moving ever so slowly so that your swing maintains rhythm and balance then it's advice that you can put to advantage. Use it but watch out for tension and surging.

An important consideration—how far is the top?

Overswinging in the backswing can lead to trouble. Some players such as John Daly can literally reach for the sky with their hands, taking their hands back and up well above the head and moving the clubshaft well past horizontal. Superior coordination and athleticism allow these players to get to impact with proper timing and on plane. However, you are better off taking the club to the top under complete control.

Here is a way to determine the proper distance for reaching the terminus or top of your backswing. Without a club, take your right hand and swing it up and back as if you were about to throw a ball. Stop at the position you would take before starting forward. Take your left arm and swing it up and back toward the right hand. The point at which the left hand stops with a comfortable stretch is the top of your backswing. You may have reached all the way to your right hand with no trouble or you may have stopped just short of it. In the latter case, bring the right hand down to meet the left hand. This is the top for you.

If you swing back beyond this natural position at the top you risk losing your balance, or especially moving the hands and arms out of a natural, supported throwing position. You then need to get your hands and arms from out of position back into position, a difficult proposition.

At the top, don't force the club beyond where your body lets it go.

— Tom Kite

HITTING FROM THE TOP

Hitting from the top features the dreaded "urge to surge," plus some other unwanted moves. From the top you should move onto the front leg first, allowing the body some natural movement forward until the weight is well onto the front foot and leg. Then the lower abdomen uncoils. This uncoiling from the abdomen unwinds the shoulders, allowing the hands a full and free release through impact.

When you hit from the top, you lunge forward with your upper body, and your arms pull your hands outside the target line. The result is a weak swing that cuts across the target line from right to left. The flight of the ball is a slice or pull without power or accuracy. The real culprit here is the arms. You're attempting to hit the ball almost entirely with the arms.

I once had a student who obviously had used the idea of pausing at the top. He eventually swung to the top, pumped downward three times, and then surged downward through the ball. It wasn't pretty, and it's the one lesson I've given in which I couldn't make a dent in this bad habit.

● No. 22

Swing the same on all shots

There is a slight variation in swing from club to club, but you should not make a conscious effort to swing one club differently than another. The natural variation is caused by the different positions in which you must stand to hit the ball for the great variety of lies encountered on any course, and the range of shaft lengths and club-head angles.

— Byron Nelson

The shorter the club, the steeper the angle of attack. The head of the iron is traveling on a steeper angle to the ball (*left*) versus a more horizontal path with the driver (*right*).

Because clubs are different lengths, the swing planes are different. Some are more upright, others more flat. The shorter the club, the steeper the angle of the shaft, the steeper or more vertical the swing plane. Club length also affects the coiling action of the body. The shorter the club, the shorter the winding of the torso. The longer the club, the longer the winding of the torso.

Ball position also accounts for slight swing variations. The ball is positioned more forward with the driver, fairway woods, and long irons. Middle and low irons are in the center of the stance.

Weight distribution changes with club selection

Shorter irons call for a proportion of the weight to be set prior to the swing on the front or left side. With the other clubs the weight is evenly distributed at setup.

When you hit shorter clubs, the focus must always couple direction and distance control. With longer clubs, especially when hitting off the tee to an expansive fairway, the focus is more on distance and less on direction.

You can't make a downswing that fully utilizes your lower body if the downswing is only slightly slower than the speed of light.

— Butch Harmon

On the other hand, the idea of swinging all clubs at the same pace has merit—a really good swing thought for most players. Unfortunately, some get the longer clubs going faster, which is not good. This is really an unconscious application of power. I will hit soft wedges, then picture the same pace and hit a 3 wood. Try it—the ball will just rocket off the face. Muscle tension tends to increase with longer clubs, so using this technique can alleviate that problem and keep you relaxed.

I like very much the concept of a free-traveling clubhead at impact. This implies that the golfer has made a full wind-up of trunk, arms and hands and used these sources of power in proper order during his downswing. The clubhead is then released to strike the ball. Many shots are spoiled at the last instant by efforts to add a few more yards. This impedes, rather than aids, the stroke. Muscles made tense in making this sudden effort hold the clubhead back.

— Bobby Jones

Drill

Swing a wedge, 5 iron, and 3 wood with your eyes closed. Do they feel the same? Doubtful! With your eyes closed, try to get a sense of rhythm and symmetry with each club that approximates the others. You may notice that the wedge swing feels shorter than the driver does, but try to establish a similar rhythm. Hit some soft wedge shots off a tee until you are contacting the ball solidly each time. Now take your 3 wood and picture the ball flying the same distance as the wedge. If you can really do this you'll be shocked by the results: rocketing +220 yard shots.

No. 23

Turn as though you were standing in a barrel

In the forward swing I have a distinct feeling that my left shoulder is moving up and my right shoulder is moving down as a consequence of my lateral leg thrust. My shoulders must return on the same relatively steep plane of their back-swing turn; I never want the feeling that they are traveling "around" instead of up and down.

— Jack Nicklaus

To Start the Body Coil, Use a Forward Press

Standing at address in a stationary position, even for a few seconds, builds muscle tension. You need to add a little motion to relieve the tension. Try a forward press, which is simply a device that helps you move from a passive position into the active stages of the swing. Try pushing with the right knee, cocking your head to the right (a movement used by Jack Nicklaus), moving the club slightly beyond or to the outside of the target line, or pressing your hands slightly to the left. These will produce a slight lateral movement of the body to the left, opposite from the big backswing movements of moving onto the back leg, coiling, and elevating your hands and arms to the top, that is, to a position that is approximately opposite or above your back shoulder, a full throwing position.

After the body and hands move to the left they come back to the right and then keep moving past the original position at address. The weight loads onto the right side, the body coils, and the hands elevate the club. The main objective is to feel how the weight moves in the golf swing. Move slightly left, then move fully onto the right foot and leg, and then back onto the left foot and leg. This subtle feel of weight movement will start giving you a sense of body rhythm and balance.

With apologies to the great teacher Percy Boomer, who first advanced this idea of swinging within an imaginary barrel up to the hips, I would say that this image works only if you're swinging in an extra wide barrel. For one thing, it gives the faulty impression of twisting and turning the body rather than coiling and stretching it.

However, one good thing about the image of swinging in a barrel is that it prevents us from moving too much from side-to-side—if we did, we'd bump against the inside of the barrel.

Otherwise, this idea has limited usefulness because the axis of the turn is not stationary. It moves. In the backswing we move the weight onto the inside of the right leg. The head and spine move with this slight lateral movement. The torso coils around the spine, which is no longer in the same position it was at address. When you coil in the backswing, think of the weight moving, not stuck to an imaginary axis at address (that would run from your original head position to the ground).

To avoid a reverse pivot in which the weight goes to the front side on the backswing and shifts to the backside on the downswing, load the weight onto the backside. When you coil in the backswing, think of the weight moving, not stuck to an imaginary axis at address.

But the serious trouble comes if we try to keep a fixed axis around which we coil and uncoil. If you don't load the weight onto the back side in the backswing you can end up creating a reverse pivot, in which the weight goes to the front side on the backswing and shifts to the back side on the downswing. This is the dreaded reverse pivot, and it is most often brought on by the effort to keep the head locked over the axis created at address.

> *Just remember the turn is a natural movement of the body . . . you will read and hear many complex instructions about the turn, but not from me.*
>
> *— Harvey Penick*

Drill

Put your left index finger on your sternum and your right hand on your belt buckle. Move into the backswing coil, moving this entire area into the inside of the your back leg and allowing the head to come along for the ride.

You should feel pressure building on the inside of your back leg, thigh muscle and up through the groin. You should also feel the front side getting stretched through the lower back and up the side. Now move this area forward into the front foot and leg and unwind the center area to a balanced finish.

IV FORWARD SWING AND IMPACT

● **No. 24**

Hold the angle, delay the hit

The term release, actually the returning of the arms and clubhead and body to the position similar to that in which they were at address, which is composed of a rotational/lateral return of the body, unhinging of the wrists and a natural return rotation of the forearms, sometimes creates controversy. There are those who don't believe such a word should exist in describing the golf swing.

— Gary Wiren

Video is one of the most useful tools for golfers and instructors. It can reveal the "unseen," it can allow me to slow down the motion to study the swings of my students, it can pause on a particular frame for closer evaluation. But it can also be detrimental when the "secrets" it reveals are misapplied.

When it comes to the advice to "hold the angle," and its kissing cousin, "delay the hit," the magic of video can turn to voodoo. Here's why. The downswing in golf is a split-second action. The action is fast and automatic. The downswing is so fast that no conscious thought, no matter how powerful, can break into and override the body's hand action, which is busy whipping the clubhead through the impact area at speeds exceeding 100 mph. For this particular swing tip, hit fast forward and move on.

Hold the angle—don't hold your breath

When you begin your movement down to the ball, you cannot—and should not—hold the angle taken when the club is in the preset or prerelease position. Even if you try to develop this technique, my question is, "When do you release it?" Actually, if the body changes direction and keeps moving, the release of the hands will feel immediate and responsive, from the top of the backswing to the finish.

My years of teaching have convinced me that there is no such thing as a cast. The player is either pulling forward with the left arm and shoulder or attempting to get the clubshaft in line with the arms "to arm the shot." However, I've had students who've simultaneously thrown the clubhead from the top and unwound the body. When this unique downswing move was viewed on videotape, it showed a full retention of leverage. I actually had a student retain more leverage throwing from the top and unwinding his body than when he was trying to hold the angle.

This downswing feel is recommended, to activate the hands and wrists rather than the arms. Jack Nicklaus once observed, "As long as your body is moving onto your left leg and through the ball, you cannot release the club too early."

So, if this idiosyncratic move is not for everyone, when should you release the hands? Video again

> **HAMMER TIME**
>
> Release the clubhead as you would drive a nail with a hammer. The right wrist cocks back and as you move the hammer forward it uncocks to strike the nail. In the golf swing, we add body movement to the right hand hammering action. When you hammer a nail, there is no conscious effort to hold the angle made when cocking the hammer.

answers the question because it shows something you cannot see with the naked eye. It shows that the angle is fully released at impact but it begins as soon as the hands are pulled below shoulder height by the change of direction of the body.

Most of the release, however, occurs as the hands drop below the hips and come alongside the rear leg deep into the hitting area. This, again, can only be seen with a video but it should not be taught as a key to a better swing. Remember, just because you can see this delayed release of the hands and wrists doesn't mean the player is consciously controlling it.

If we allow the right hand to take hold at the very beginning of the downstroke, we are hitting too soon. The swing hasn't a chance to get started in the right groove, and the power is apt to be spent too soon; the wrists will have been uncocked before the stored-up energy can be expended upon the ball.

— Bobby Jones

Started with Hogan

I believe a lot of people watched video of Ben Hogan's swing and saw the hands and wrists coming down alongside his body still in the cocked position. He had tremendous power stored in this "clubhead lag." Hogan was, however, concentrating on moving his body forward and uncoiling his torso. He was not thinking about keeping his wrists cocked, or holding the angle. The downswing is a race in which the body gets a head start. The arms, hands, and club eventually catch up with the body, and the race ends in a dead heat at impact.

Hogan explained it this way: "The hands do nothing active until after the arms have moved on the downswing to a position just above the level of the hips. The arms don't propel this motion themselves. They are carried down by the movement of the hips. The correct hitting motion is one unbroken thrust from the beginning of the downswing to the end of the follow-through."

Hogan, I'm sure, did not think of these actions as two separate movements—lower body movement and releasing the hands—but rather one continuous movement.

The origin of this teaching concept springs from looking at a single, stop-action frame of a swing motion and drawing the wrong conclusions. It's a

YOU CANNOT PUT YOURSELF IN A DELAYED RELEASE POSITION

Golf instructor David Leadbetter advocates holding the angle, but it's noteworthy that he stresses the idea that "you cannot just put yourself in the delayed release position; it's a moment captured in a series of good movements and so can only be achieved in conjunction with a correctly moving body."

prime example of a movement that can be proven through video observation but should not be recognized as something to teach. This is analogous to teaching a pitcher how to throw a baseball. Pitching coaches never emphasize thrusting the elbow ahead of the hand (holding the angle) and then releasing it as it passes the shoulder. Rather, they teach the pitcher to keep the arm relaxed and elbow up and allow the natural throwing motion to place the elbow forward of the hand. The same applies to the golf swing—just let the swing flow and trust your natural athleticism to properly order the sequence of motions.

Delay the hit

This one is related closely to "hold the angle." But at least in this phrase there is an implied release or hit.

According to the proponents of delaying the hit, this advice allows the lower body to make the initial move forward to the ball while the hands trail behind. The wrists remain fully cocked until at least halfway through the downswing. The hips are then able to rotate, clearing a path for the hands to travel uninhibited to the ball. "Delaying the hit" will also guard a golfer from using the arms as the power source. The right wrist must remain in a cocked throwing position until about waist high in the downswing. From here it can pour it on through the hitting area.

Hold it with your left hand so you can hit it as hard as you can with your right hand and not hook it.

— Tommy Bolt

The club is released in one continuous motion as soon as the hands are pulled below the shoulder height by the change of direction of the body. Release the clubhead as you would drive a nail with a hammer.

Upon closer examination

Thanks to high-speed, stop-action photography and video, this all makes sense, but it begs the question, "Is it practical to teach?" For one thing, the hands—which remain cocked until they drop below the shoulders—cannot be consciously manipulated at the speed they're traveling. And thinking about delaying the hit runs the risk of disrupting timing and rhythm. Many golfers react to this idea by decelerating the club in the downswing. The arms, which start the delay, have to slow down even further to provide

The hands and arms remain passive as the body changes direction into the front foot and leg.

any chance of delivering the clubhead squarely at impact.

Delaying the hit also means manipulating the hands through the hitting area. Getting the clubface squared to the target line is difficult, but when you add the task of delaying the hit you're flirting with frustration and failure. It's true that the hands are the fastest part of the body and capable of adjustments on the fly, but they're also hard-pressed to consistently arrive at the same place at the same time. The result is that they arrive late on one swing and early on another. The former produces a push to the right and the latter a pull or pull-hook to the left. It's no way to run a golf game!

She worked with her teacher on the roll of the right hand through the hitting area. I think it was one of the greatest things about her swing and I don't think many people know that.

— LPGA Founder Marilynn Smith, commenting on Mickey Wright, LPGA Hall of Fame member

Drill

Hitting chip shots, take the club back to waist high and move into and through the ball with the body. Let the hands catch up and sting the ball. This is a drill that emphasizes athleticism and coordination—work the right hand to square the clubface while the body is moving. Vary this drill by swinging the right hand/right arm only—slap or spank the ball. Then swing left hand/left arm only and slap the ball away with the back of the left hand facing the target.

No. 25

Hit down on the ball

Let the clubhead continue through the ball low
along the ground on the line to the target.

— *Gene Littler*

Hitting down on the ball sounds logical! There really is no other way to approach the ball with the clubhead. We are standing above the ball. The clubhead is taken back and up in the backswing. How else would you approach the ball once the clubhead is poised above your shoulders at the top of the backswing?

Yes, you do hit down but you also hit through the ball. When a player focuses on the idea, "hit down on the ball," he or she inevitably makes a chopping swing. The player lifts the club up, as you would take back an ax to split a log, then chops down with a wristy swing that risks missing the ball

Yes, you do hit down on the ball but you also hit through the ball extending the club down the target line as it moves through the impact area.

FOCUS ON COILING

Regrettably, misinterpretation of the instruction "pull down with the left hand" can start the golfer on the path of "hitting down on the ball." Golfers misinterpret this advice by starting the downswing with a conscious pull with the left hand and arm from the top. This throws the swing out of sequence. Forget pulling from the top. To get into the proper ballstriking position, focus on coiling into the back leg and uncoiling into the front foot and leg. The uncoiling brings the arms and hands down and alongside the body. As they pass down and by the right hip, the unwinding of the torso pulls them through the impact zone while the wrists uncock and square the clubface. The correct clubhead path is down and then along the target line, not straight down as when pulled from the top.

altogether. Instead, the result at worst is a club imbedded in the turf a few inches behind the ball still resting in place, and at best a ball lofted in a weak, soft arc well short of the desired distance.

Staying down to the ball means keeping the body, rather than just the hand, down through the hitting area,

— *Byron Nelson*

The idea of hitting down on the ball can also promote a shortened follow-through. The chopping swing often buries the club in the ground. Players make an incorrect swing to the ball and not a correct swing through the ball.

The majority of players hit their iron shots badly because they are afraid of hitting down. . . . These players keep their weight back on the right leg and try to scoop the ball up. That's the cause of most topped iron shots and plowing up the turf before the ball is hit.

— *Tommy Armour*

Drill

Place a ball on a tee and then place a second tee 4 inches directly in front of the ball at the same height as the tee holding the ball. Set up to the ball using a 7 iron. When you swing, focus on the forward tee and try to get your right hand to hit the forward tee with the clubhead. This will get you using your right side (the extender on the forward swing) and get you hitting through the ball.

● No. 26

Extend the arms and hands toward the target on the through swing

I can't think of anything worse to do with a golf club in your hands than "accelerate and follow through." Does the swing accelerate? Yes. What's making it accelerate? Gravity. . . . Is there a follow-through? Of course there is. Why? Because of the swing, because of momentum . . . If you think "accelerate and follow through" when you swing, then you are going to try to help momentum. Believe me, momentum doesn't need any help.

— *Martin Hall*

Trouble arises when we misinterpret this advice to extend the arms on the through swing by forgetting about the full extension of the right arm in the through swing and follow-through. At impact and slightly beyond impact the left arm extends and then folds after the swing moves through the striking area.

As the left arm folds or bends, it collapses so that the elbow points toward the ground and the left wrist is under the shaft. Just beyond impact the right arm is fully extended with the back of the hand and forearm in line, a position that is very much similar to the position of the left arm at the top of the backswing. The player's weight is almost entirely on his left foot, while the inside edge of the ball of the right foot is on the ground. The hips have turned so that they are facing the target.

Right hand is leader of the smack

The most important thing to understand about extension is that it is created by the movement of the right side of the body. It is the extender on the

To get the feel of the left arm folding, swing the club with the left arm only (1 and 2).
To get the feel of right hand extension, swing the club with the right hand only. With your
left hand, grab your right front pocket and pull it toward the target with the right hand
(3 and 4).

through swing just as the left side is the extender on the backswing. To achieve extension into, through, and past impact, the right side—particularly the right hand—must actively deliver the strike of the clubhead into the back of the ball. It must be the leader of the smack.

Hands finish high?

An erroneous corollary to this idea is to finish with your hands high in the follow-through, but as a general rule governing the finish of the swing, the higher the hands and arms at the finish, the more weight still resting on your right foot. And the higher you swing the arms the less you can rotate the torso.

The correct follow-through and finish require that you unwind your body to a full, balanced finish (remember that in the downswing the head initially moves slightly down and forward before moving up to a full finish). In the follow-through the head follows the body, which moves forward into the front foot and leg and eventually past the original position at address and up.

Keep body moving

Extension through the ball is a function of the unwinding of the body around the front foot and leg as well as the delivery of the club with the right hand. If the body stops or isn't moving through the ball, the hands must go to the left of where you want them to go. The results: pulls or weak slices.

Drill

Take the club back halfway to a throwing position. With your left hand grab your right hip pocket. Pull the right pocket forward through the ball and naturally and simultaneously toss the clubhead toward the target with your right hand. You can actually toss the club (as long as you have room). No broken windows, please!

● No. 27

Stay behind the ball

*The good player swings through the ball while
the awkward player hits at it.*

— *Ken Venturi*

When a player hits short and middle irons, the head is closest to being aligned with the ball at impact. That is, when we look at the player face on, or from the side, the head is positioned along a line that runs perpendicular to and intersects the target line at the back of the ball. With longer irons and the driver your head is slightly behind the ball at impact. But you need to chase after the ball after contact. You must allow your body to release. Just after impact, the unwinding of the shoulders should allow the head to rotate with the shoulders and to come up out of the shot. Any effort to keep the head and right shoulder back behind the ball after the point of contact will cause the weight to stay on the back leg. This error will shut down the power of your swing and cause pulls, pull hooks, and push fades.

Every golf swing ultimately finishes forward of the point of impact. The shoulders turn about 200 degrees on the forward swing, actually catching up and passing the hips just after impact. At the finish of the swing, the chest faces slightly left of a line parallel to the target line and the hips face directly down this line.

Common fault/wrong cure

Players sometimes feel that their body is ahead of the ball in the swing and try correcting this by staying behind the ball. They're going down the wrong road. What's really happening—where the real trouble is—is that the clubhead is behind the hands at impact. So if you're hitting driver or fairway woods to the right, you might try focusing on your right hand. When the body moves forward of the ball prior to impact, the swing is in the left side too long. The fault is not that you are ahead of the ball. The fault is that your right hand and right side are late kicking into action. Instead, move into and through the ball, involving your right hand and right side to hit the ball away.

If you are trying to stay behind the ball and, as a result, hitting fat or thin shots, you're probably doing a good job of what you set out to do. Stop it! Move through the ball and let your right hand do some work. Start subscribing to Tommy Armour's thoughts: "Hold the club with your left hand and smack the hell out of the ball with your right hand."

An erroneous corollary to the idea of staying behind the

At the finish the right side finishes past the ball. You must allow the body to release to achieve both solid contact and accuracy.

ball is the idea of not letting your body or hands get ahead of the club. This is wrong. The body is always leading the club until the hands swing it past the body after impact. The ideal action in a swing is to have the body, hands, and club go through the ball—at impact—together. However, the body is always ahead of the club on the downswing and the hands lead the club all the way down until the club catches up with the ball at impact.

Drill

This is a drill using the right hand only. Start with a wedge, hitting the ball off a tee and then progress to where you can hit the ball off the turf, right hand only. Progress to other clubs until you can eventually hit the driver.

● No. 28

Hit against a firm left side

When I feel that the bulk of my weight has been transferred to my left side—actually it hasn't been, but it feels that way for every golfer—then I want my left hip to brake its forward motion. I do this by firming my left leg with a conscious movement—firming the left knee. The left leg becomes almost straight but it retains its flexibility. This act of firming the left leg forces the left hip to rotate to the rear—what is commonly called "clearing the left side."

— Jack Nicklaus

The image conveyed by this tip is that of a player stopping the uncoiling of his body after he starts the downswing, holding the left side rigid, and then hitting past it. Hitting against a firm left side is a myth. No good golfer ever does it. Rather, the left side moves steadily to the left on the downswing and then turns away from the directional line of the shot. A better idea is to think of hitting against a firm left leg. This also implies that there is a hit, which must come from the right hand.

Movement of the left side

The left side, in a good swing, starts and stays far ahead of the club. It is always pulling and stretching, always generating a feeling of tension. Taut and stretched out, the left side is moved far out of the way of the downswinging arms. These arms and hands do not hit against the left side. The left side gets out of the way so the arms and hands can hit through toward the target.

The left leg, however, must straighten through impact to allow the body to unwind freely. Only when the left side is out of the way can the full, free

The left leg must straighten through impact to allow the body to unwind freely. Strike the ball with your right hand (2 and 3).

speed of the club ever be generated. Throughout the hitting zone and at impact, the right side trails the left side but moves through the ball as the right hand delivers the clubhead.

Drill

Stand alongside a kitchen counter with your left hip approximately 1 inch away. Take your right hand back just past waist high, allowing your weight to move slightly to your right foot. Now drive into your front foot and leg and pretend you are slapping something away with your right hand. You should be able to move aggressively into and around your left leg without your left hip bumping the counter as you actively slap, spank, or throw your right hand toward the counter.

Stand behind a chair and take your hand back as if you're taking a club to the "at-the-top" position (1). Drive into your front leg and pretend you are slapping something with your right hand (2). You should make this move without toppling the chair.

Although both sides of your body play significant roles in your golf swing, they do so at different times. True, more emphasis should be placed on the left side as you start down. But then, at about the halfway stage, the right side of your body must take the leading role. Assuming you are in the correct hitting position, you can fire through the ball as hard as you like with your powerful right side.

— David Leadbetter

● No. 29

Drive the legs toward the target

As you shift your lower body (and weight) forward remember that this move must start from the ground up. As your hips continue to turn, your weight follows and shifts across the outside of your left foot and into your left heel, which is where it is at impact.

— Hank Haney

I'd be the first to advocate some kind of leg drive in order to transfer the body's weight onto the front side and set up for the uncoiling of the torso. But this adage can get you into all kinds of trouble if you move the legs too far forward and they get out from under the upper body. Then they can't support the body's movement. The so-called leg drive is better envisioned and thought of as a movement toward the target with the body. This brings the weight onto the front side in a more controlled move. Once the body drives into the front foot and leg, the torso unwinds into and against a stable front leg.

If the lateral movement is not made, the weight stays back and power is lost. The swing bottoms out prior to reaching the ball, creating thin, tipped, and fat shots. Further consequences: If you hang back and do not move laterally toward the target—thus failing to transfer your weight forward—you will move the arc of the swing outside the line of flight. Good, powerful shots result from the ball being struck along the target line. An outside, right-to-left approach of the swing path yields weak, ineffective shots.

Because the hips are turned to the right on the backswing, players often think that the next movement is simply turning the hips to the left. This is wrong. You need to move the hips and body laterally to the left until your weight is inside the left leg, then uncoil the torso and hips. Thus, the leg drive is actually the movement that brings the hips and torso forward so the torso can unwind and the arms, wrists, and hands can release themselves through the hitting zone.

Because the hips are turned to the right on the backswing, players often think that the next movement is simply turning the hips to the left. This is wrong. Move the hips and body laterally to the left until your weight is inside the left leg (1). The hips begin to unwind (2). The body rotates or uncoils through impact against a firm left leg (3).

Drill

Put both hands on your abdomen, one hand below your belt and one hand above. Make a little coil into your back leg and then drive your center slightly downward into the left foot and leg. Your left leg will move somewhat forward to support the drive of the body. The main feel is to drive the weight downward to the inside of the foot.

● **No. 30**

Pull down with your left arm; the left arm controls the swing

The hips initiate the downswing. They are the pivotal element in the chain reaction. Starting them first and moving them correctly—this one action practically makes the downswing.

— Ben Hogan

This idea of pulling down with your left arm, if strictly followed without assistance and some kind of coordination with the rest of the body, will shut down the centrifugal force that propels the clubhead. That's because when the arm works alone, that is, not part of a sequence of motions, as this idea unfortunately suggests, you cannot build speed. And you're left with no power to strike the ball. At best, shots that are struck by pulling down or through with the left arm will fly weakly to the right.

Picture a baseball batter swinging at a pitch without the hips opening and the torso unwinding. The lead arm (the left arm for a right-handed batter) would gradually straighten just beyond the point of contact. But the bat would transmit very little energy to the ball. In fact, a major league fastball at 95 mph would likely knock the bat from the batter's hand. Everything is wrong with this picture. There is no speed on the barrelhead, minimal transfer of energy to the ball upon contact and absolutely no chance of knocking the ball beyond the infielders. Put it in the book—you're out, every time!

During the downswing I make no conscious effort to restrain my hands, arms or shoulders. I want them to move as freely and fast as possible, providing they follow my lower-body actions.

— Jack Nicklaus

In the golf swing you suffer similar consequences when you pull down or forward with the left arm without coordinating this with the coiling action of the legs, hips, and torso. You need more than the arm pulling the head of the club forward or down. And you will get into trouble by isolating on this action. You need more if you hope to hit the ball with any success.

Integrate this idea

You need the uncoiling of the back and side muscles of the torso, which creates a centrifugal pulling action. The lower center of the body, the hips, and the lower left side of the back move into the left foot and then rotate around

As you complete the backswing (1) and start the downswing (2) you need more than the left arm pulling the head of the club forward or down. You need the body to change direction into the front foot and leg. Once into the leg the body begins to unwind, which pulls the hands and arms downward into the hitting position.

PULL IS FROM THE LEFT SIDE, NOT FROM THE LEFT ARM

There is pull from the left side in a good golf swing, but not from the left arm. In the backswing, the muscles across the lower back and up the left side are stretched. These muscles extend through the shoulder and down the arm.

In the change of direction, the body moves into the front foot and leg, maintaining stretch. As the lower left side unwinds around the inside of the left leg and hip, this stretch increases. Any independent pulling action from the left arm and shoulder eliminates this stretch, causing a brownout in power. Additionally, this pulling action from the left tends to move the hands and clubhead outside the target line leading to pulls and weak slices. Keep in mind that if you emphasize the pull from the left side, you also need some awareness of the delivery or strike of the club with the right hand and right side.

the left leg. The upper body follows, and as the body uncoils it builds up speed in the arms and hands, and ultimately in the clubhead. You can now deliver the clubhead to the back of the ball and send it on its way.

Think of the action during the downswing and through swing as the arms and hands being moved by movement of the legs, hips, and torso muscles. The lower body and torso initiate the downswing and the uncoiling brings the arms, hands, and clubhead into motion. The arms, hands, and clubhead are propelled to high speeds by centrifugal force.

When you extend your left arm back feel how the muscles in the left upper arm and upper left side (back and shoulder) increase their stretch.

Drill

Extend your left arm back and feel the muscles in your left side stretch.
Put your right hand under your left elbow. Now move into your front foot
and leg with your body and simultaneously push your left arm back. Feel
how the muscles in the left side increase their stretch. This is the ideal
in the change of direction.

No. 31

Fire the right knee when striking the ball, especially on pitch shots

*I found a way to play fairly effectively with one
swing thought, but I almost never played well if
I had two. Forget three.*

— *Raymond Floyd*

This advice is definitely an important piece of the swing puzzle. I believe I've
heard TV golf analyst Ken Venturi, for one, speak about how he triggers the
return to the ball when hitting pitch shots by firing his right knee. It works,
too. Venturi can land and stop a 90-yard pitch on the hood of a car. But I think
he would agree that it's a personal key that enables him to unlock the entire
right side and get it moving into the shot.

You definitely want to get from the back side (right leg) to the front side
(left leg) in the downswing and through swing, and moving the right knee
helps accomplish this. However, when students hear, "Fire the right knee,"
they are often left with the impression that it's only the right knee that moves

Move the entire right side of the body, and the right hip can act as a trigger. The desired result is to get the weight over on the left side as you hit through the ball and finish the shot.

forward. You want to move the entire right side of the body, and the right knee can act as a trigger. I feel a much better swing thought is to move the right hip and right hand together through the ball.

I teach my students to imagine the entire right side going over along with the right hip. The desired result is to get the weight over on the left side as you hit through the ball and finish the shot.

In my own game I have problems related to this movement. If I fire my right knee forward it leaves very little for pushing off the right side or foot and thus moving the entire right side through the shot. For me, firing the right knee leads to moving it too abruptly, to pushing it out from under my body, and to driving it too far forward of the right shoulder. Thus, the right shoulder and right hip lag behind. Result? My entire right side drops too far down and back. You can understand why I am cautious about literally firing the right knee to initiate the downswing.

Kick starting the rotating motion

Lateral body motion serves to kick-start the rotary motion in the downswing, which lowers the swing plane and gives the right hand a better opportunity to square the clubface at impact. To accomplish this I think of initiating my swing by rocking the right knee forward, which allows a more rhythmic and flowing movement to start the backswing. For me, everything on the right side flows into and through the ball. The result is that I do not move too far down or back in the downswing.

What I like about the advice to initiate the downswing by

Practice putting your left hand on your right pocket and pulling to feel the right side fire.

rocking the right knee forward is that it gets you thinking about the proper action of the right side in the swing, which is to move forward from its position at the conclusion of the backswing and turn into the shot. This helps make you execute the shot correctly and gets you to move not only the knee but also the right hip and upper torso—the entire right side—into the shot.

Drills

Put your left hand on your right pocket and pull. Allow yourself to turn and face the target with your sternum. Note that your right shoulder does not dip or lower itself significantly. This is the action you should incorporate into your swing.

Here is another drill that can help you move the right side into the swing without the notion of firing the right knee. Take your normal stance setup and place a club on the ground 4 inches forward of your right instep. Hit some iron shots, focusing on starting down and forward by shifting the right knee and hip in front of the shaft on the ground. Do not just fire the right knee. Rather, glide both the knee and hip forward and push forward with the inside of the right foot, getting the entire right side moving as the knee moves forward. Remember, shift the knee, hip, and entire right side, then rotate to finish the swing. This will correctly lower the club into position for a slightly inside and then square-to-the-target-line approach to the ball.

WORK THE ANKLES

Jack Grout was Jack Nicklaus's teacher and coach, and he had a useful way of looking at the initiation of the downswing. He didn't recommend focusing on the right knee: he believed that the knees would follow correctly if you worked the ankles. Here is what he recommended: "On the backswing, your left ankle rolls inward toward your right foot so that most of your weight shifts from left to right onto the inside of the right foot (the rest remaining on the inside of the left). Then, at the start of the downswing, both ankles roll laterally to the left so your weight gradually shifts from the inside of your right foot to the inside of your left foot."

Here I would prefer to emphasize footwork, with the weight moving to the inside of the right foot in the backswing and driving down into the inside of the left foot as you change direction. The body is moving, coiling, driving, and unwinding, and the feet give the body support and rhythm.

● No. 32

Roll your top hand over the bottom hand in the forward swing

> *The hands must hit past the body, not with the body. Through impact the left hand gradually turns down and over as the right hand hits past it. The action is a rolling or turning of the hands, not an inward collapsing of the left wrist or a forward bending of the right wrist.*
>
> *— Henry Cotton*

We needed a little high-tech help in setting this one straight.

Special thanks to Charles Hulcher, inventor of today's modern high-speed, stop-action, 35-mm camera technology, which captures the golf swing frame by frame in thousandths of a second. His technology has enabled us to see the hands at work throughout the swing. It reveals that prior to, during, and at impact there is no rolling of the wrists, one over the other.

The hands and wrists are active during the swing (more on this below) but the positional relationship between the top and bottom hands remains relatively the same in a well-executed swing.

At address the right hand rests over or on top of the left hand and the lower part of the right arm is above the left arm. When the club goes back in the takeaway and up in the backswing, the wrists hinge or cock. If the backswing is executed properly at the top, the left wrist is relatively flat and the right wrist is bent back in a throwing position. On the downswing the wrists uncock, returning the hands to the same position at address: the palm of the right hand and the back of the left hand aligned, that is, parallel with the face of the club.

This allows the clubface to be returned at impact square or perpendicular to the target line. The hands have not rolled—they're opposing each other, keeping the clubface moving down the target line through impact.

What the baseball swing can teach you

The action in the golf swing, with the hands or palms opposing each other, is very similar to the impact position when hitting a baseball. When a baseball is struck correctly, say waist high, the palms are in a top hand/palm up, bottom hand/palm down position. The wrists have cocked and uncocked but the top hand has not rolled over the bottom hand. If you were to overlay a baseball player's impact position in meeting a waist-high fastball with hitting a ball with the end of the bat off the turf, you would see a position nearly identical to the golf swing position at impact.

The baseball analogy is further useful. In a baseball swing, if the right hand prematurely rolls over the left, it moves the barrel out of the way of the pitch. It actually raises it and causes the ball to be struck on its upper hemisphere. The result is a ground ball to the batter's pull side of the playing field.

In golf, if the right hand prematurely rolls over the left—at impact or just prior to impact—the clubface closes. The swing then loses full extension; that

The right hand and clubhead square up to the ball long before impact (1). At impact the hands have not rolled—they're opposing each other, keeping the clubface moving down the target line through impact (2).

is, the rolling of the top hand forces the premature folding of the left arm, thus reducing the arc of the swing (and the swing's velocity and power). The result with a driver in-hand off the tee would be at best a 125-yard duck hook and at worst a 75-yard "worm burner" down the left side of the fairway.

The unhinging action of the wrists—which squares the clubhead at impact—is an important source of power. Any rolling action of the hands, wrists, or lower arms diminishes this power. Here is a way you can demonstrate to yourself the magnitude of the power outage that the rolling of the top hand over the bottom hand at impact can cause.

Slowly swing your club and stop it at the impact position. Next, have a buddy hold the clubhead in place. Try moving the clubhead forward by rolling the top hand. The action is weak and if you're able to move the clubhead at all, it's moving left, off the target line. Now try uncocking the wrists, palms opposing each other, back and forward, down the target line. You can feel the superior power and strength this hand position and wrist action yield. If you need further assurance, ask your buddy which of the two movements made it more difficult to hold the club in place.

Eyes fool us

So if we know upon closer examination—via the use of high-speed, stop action photography—and analysis that the action of rolling your wrists at impact is a myth, why does this misconception persist? I think it's because our eyes fool us when we view the hand action during the front swing as the club and hands move past the impact area and upward to waist height and beyond.

After impact the clubhead moves down the target line only a few inches and then starts moving off the target line and closer to the body. During this through swing and follow-through the wrists hinge toward the body, which is what our eyes see and misinterpret as a rolling of the wrists. Rather, the arms and hands are acting to control the clubhead that has been freewheeling down the target line. It now must be decelerated and brought back around the body. Throughout, the player makes no conscious effort to roll the top hand over the left. His last conscious movement with the hands in the downswing is their unhinging (from their position at the top) to square the clubface at impact. Because so many players leave the club open through impact, the feel of closing the clubface or rolling the right hand over the left arm is a good feel to practice to learn to square the clubface and draw the ball.

Drill

Here is a drill to help you ingrain the proper hand position at impact and avoid rolling your wrists. Swing a club approximately 3 feet back and then 3 feet past the impact point. On the backswing cock the wrists slightly and work the club back until the left arm is extended (approximately 3 feet from the ball). Move your weight onto the inside of your rear leg and gently coil the torso. Then uncoil and swing the club back through the impact area, unhinging the wrists and striking the ball.

Continue the swing approximately 3 three feet beyond impact, at least until the top hand and arm are fully extended. At the finish of this swing you should be able to just barely see the fingers of your top hand (right hand) and the clubface. If you can see them you have not rolled your wrists. Congratulations—mission accomplished!

No. 33

Return to the address position at impact

A correct impact is one where the club is coming into the ball from the inside with the clubface square to the arc of the swing.

— Hank Haney

How this idea ever gained favor is a mystery. Common sense tells you this isn't the case. At address the player is motionless, the weight is evenly distributed on each foot, both feet are firmly planted on the ground, and the hips are parallel to the target line. At impact, the hips are opened to the target line, just slightly forward of the position taken at the stance. Nearly every part of the body is moving, approximately 80 percent of the weight is on the left foot, and the heel of the right foot is raised slightly. The right shoulder has lowered and moved forward of its position at address.

The impact position is dynamic—you reach it and leave it in a split second. The big muscles of the back and legs are propelling the arms, wrists, and hands—and the clubhead—through the impact area. The address position is static—nothing is moving and you are not building any force or momentum.

One of the most common faults I see on the lesson tee is a swing that gears down and, in some cases, stops in the impact area. The body literally

Place your club against the bottom of your bag (1). Next, move into your front foot and leg, putting pressure into the clubshaft so that it flexes (2). This should give you a feel of how the legs and body transfer energy into the shaft of the club, which is unlike the feeling you have at address.

RETURN ADDRESS

Returning the clubshaft to the ball at the same angle it made at address is a good way to produce consistent shots. It indicates that you've squared the clubface on the downswing, and that you've made an approach angle that is appropriate for the club (shallow for woods, steeper for irons).

Ben Hogan, who endeavored to master returning the clubshaft at the same angle of address, actually returned his club slightly under the imaginary plane created by his takeaway. Players such as Nick Price, however, bring their clubshafts back to the ball on the downswing at the same angle taken at address. But no players try to recreate the address position in its entirety at impact.

slows or stops at precisely the moment it should be moving into and through the ball. The result is poor contact. If the body isn't moving into and through the ball, the club bottoms out prior to impact, thus producing topped, thin, and fat shots.

> *Most players' hands instinctively return to*
> *the same alignment at impact that they were in*
> *at address.*
>
> — *Henry Cotton*

Drill

Assume your address position and place the face of your club against something solid, such the tire of a golf cart or, if you're trying this at home, the foot of a sofa. Now move into your front foot and leg; put pressure into the clubshaft so that it flexes. You should be pushing off your right foot and the hands should stay close to the inside of the right thigh. You should start to get a feel of dynamic impact and a sense of how the legs and body transfer pressure and energy into the shaft of the club. This is unlike the static position taken at address.

● No. 34

Extend both arms at impact

At the moment of impact most players come up too quickly with the body and head, following the turn of the left shoulder. The better player stays down through the hitting area much longer with his body by keeping his knees flexed, his left side leading and his head back. The right side comes down and under instead of up and around, and the clubhead trajectory is as low as possible, following the ball as it goes through the shot.

— Byron Nelson

This is oh-so-close to being a great swing thought but unfortunately it needs some tweaking. Most importantly, you need to understand that the arms are fully extended just past impact, not precisely at impact.

At impact, the right arm and wrist are slightly bent and the left arm is fully extended. Slightly past the striking point, both arms are fully extend. This position is the result of a series of correct movements, including the movements of the lower body, torso, arms, and hands. It is the result of a sequence of movements that allowed the body to fully extend the arms at the right moment.

Trouble from the start

Some players get into trouble by trying to get into this fully extended position from the start. They line up at address with both the arms extended, stiff and full of tension. This leads to a swing that is all arms and club and not very much body. Their swings lack dynamic action of the body.

They don't realize that the arm is not extended at address the same way it is extended at impact and that the arm is not swung like a bar, fully extended throughout the movement.

Some of my students tighten their arms as they come into the ball—they're trying to control the clubface. It's similar to slamming on the brakes of an accelerating car. You need to step on the accelerator when coming into the ball, not hit the brakes. The squaring of the club is accomplished reflexively—the clubface is delivered along the target line with the hands opposed at impact as part of the fast-moving continuum of lower and upper body swing action. It is not independently manipulated to a square position.

The club has freedom in the striking area, the freedom to explode into the back of the ball as the clubhead is released by the arms, wrists, and hands. Control comes from making the correct coiling and uncoiling of the body. It comes from making the approach to the ball with the clubface square or perpendicular to your intended target line and a sense of the clubhead moving directly into the back of the ball.

Past impact, your right forearm should be crossing over your left. The clubhead will be flashing rapidly to the left of the target line as the follow-through continues. Many amateurs believe that they must keep the clubhead on the target line after impact. This thought only leads to a blocking action through impact, and is the cause of so many shots that are hit well right of the target.

— Butch Harmon

The arms are not extended at address (1) the same way they are extended at impact (2).
The club has freedom in the striking area, the freedom to explode into the back of the ball.

Drill

Take that ax out of the woodshed and go chop down a tree. Notice how the

clear intention of delivering the ax into the tree extends the arms. Notice

also that the drive of the body up through the feet adds power. You're using

everything you've got to send the head of the ax into the tree.

The swing begins with a well-balanced and athletic setup (1). The player emits a sense of strength and energy that will enable him to hit the ball hard. The takeaway (2) has an early movement into the back leg; it begins as the club moves the initial two feet back and up. As the club works up (3), the body coils into the back leg and hip. As the body windup nears completion (4), the base or lower body is solid and the hands are in a strong launch position, ready to hit. When fully loaded (5) the hands are ready and the torso is coiled. As the body changes direction by moving into the front leg and foot the hands and arms remain relatively passive (6). As the hands move down past the waist the right side and right hand get moving into action. The left side braces and right side and right hand—clubface square to the target line at impact—pour through the impact area make a full and free strike of the ball (8–10). The right side continues moving past the ball, the head and eyes up to watch its flight (11). A good finish has the right shoulder closer than the left shoulder to the target and a straight up-and-down spine (12).

The objective of the player is not to swing the club in a specified manner, nor to execute a series of complicated movements in a prescribed sequence, not to look pretty while he is doing it, but primarily and essentially to strike the ball with the head of the club so that the ball will perform according to his wishes.

No one can play golf until he knows the many ways in which a golf ball can be expected to respond when it is struck in different ways. If you think that all this should be obvious, please believe me when I assure you that I have seen many really good players attempt shots they should have known were impossible.

— Bobby Jones

Striking Action of the Hands

There is a need to understand the natural striking action of the hands. If I were to hit something with the back of my left hand, such as batting a tennis ball or smacking a rug hanging from a clothesline, the left arm would be fully extended and slightly firmed up upon contact. After contact, the left arm and wrist would relax and bend outward toward the direction the ball was propelled. However, when the right hand reaches the striking point, alone or joined together with the left hand, the right arm and wrist at contact are slightly bent backward (away from the direction the ball is flying), forming an angle of perhaps 15 to 20 degrees. The action of the right hand is that of spanking or slapping the ball. When you hit a golf ball, your arms extend in response to the hitting action of the right hand through the ball and the full, free release of the clubhead with the body in motion. The actual point of full extension is slightly beyond the contact point with the ball.

V PUTTING

● No. 35

Hit fast putts on the toe of the putter

The man who can putt is a match
for anyone.

— Willie Park Jr.

Slippery, downhill putts test the nerves of any golfer. And when you add a side-hill break to a downhill roll it makes it hard to bring the putter back and through—you think, "When I hit this, will it ever stop rolling if it misses the cup?"

To hit a fast-rolling putt, you need to stroke the ball and keep the clubface square. What you don't need is an explosive pop stroke, an accelerating stroke, or a long backstoke and follow-through, any of which will add too much energy to the ball. What to do?

One popular method is to hit the ball on the toe of your putter. This definitely transfers less energy but it can also cause the putter head to twist and thus start the putt off line. With such a technique, the way to keep the putter head square is to tighten the hands on the grip. This adds tension to a situation that already has you listening to the sound of your heart beating against your chest.

The overwhelming majority of
unsuccessful putts are missed not
because they were misjudged but
because they were mishit.

— Jackie Burke Jr.

The key to successfully hitting extremely fast putts is to keep a steady, rhythmic stroke while at the same time applying less force. Here is one way to accomplish that. Grip down on the putter so that your right hand is almost touching the shaft. This naturally shortens the arc, slightly slows the stroke, and allows you to transfer less energy to the ball. Now, when you stroke the ball on the sweet spot, it will stay on line.

If a putt looks straight, don't stare at the line for a long period of time trying to see if there's something you overlooked. Sooner or later, you'll invent a break that isn't there.

— Corey Pavin

USE THE TOE TO LESSEN THE BLOW

Not everyone agrees that toed putts should be forsaken for choking up on the grip. PGA instructor Todd Sones feels that it's a technique worth mastering: "In order to combat the dangers of a fast downhill putt, many players set up to strike the putt on the toe of the putter rather than on the sweet spot. Hitting the ball on the toe will help deaden the putt. A ball hit on the toe will roll far less than a putt hit in the center with the same stroke. So instead of making a tiny tap on the ball (which is difficult to execute with accuracy under intense pressure) players will toe their putts. The softer roll is typically easier to control and usually produces the best results. Toed putts come in handy not only on downhill putts but on those severe left-to-right and right-to-left sliders."

If you decide to put the toed putts in your arsenal, just remember the following tips. You should stroke the ball, not tap it. This will give you the ability to make a positive movement and not a tentative one. And be sure to push your hands together to give the putter more stability—it will not torque, or turn, which is the greatest detriment to a straight and true stroke.

If you move the ball toward the toe of your putter (*center*) on a fast downhill path, it will help deaden the contact. Control the distance by aiming for a spot 3 to 4 feet short of the hole (*right*) and letting the ball drift the rest of the way to the hole.

● No. 36

Never up, never in

I work to the rule that if the green appears to be fast, I will aim my putt at an imaginary hole six to twelve inches short of the hole. If the green appears to be slow, and particularly if during the last two or three feet to the hole the ground is uphill, I hit it firmly for the back of the hole.

— Bobby Locke

Speed is very important in putting. Regardless of how well you've determined the line, if you don't strike the ball with the proper speed you'll miss the hole. The common advice, "Never up, never in," which calls for a stroke that keeps up the speed of the putt as it approaches the cup, often compounds the problem of holing it.

Short-game guru Dave Pelz recommends that you roll your putts with speed sufficient to bring the ball to rest an optimum 17 inches past the hole (assuming the hole is covered when the ball rolls over it). Pelz's advice is based on research that shows the ball needs enough speed to help it traverse what he terms "the lumpy doughnut" that encircles the cup.

The doughnut, he explains, is the result of players not walking too close to the cup when retrieving balls from the cup. Their feet tamp down the greens a foot or so from the cup but not the area closest to the cup. Putts are usually slowing down as they reach this doughnut area. Pelz feels that as putts get close to the hole (just as they're slowing down), they need speed to run up the ramp into the hole. The lesson taught at the Pelz School of Putting is familiar: "Never up, never in."

It's true, if the ball doesn't get to the hole it has no chance of falling in. But when we think consciously of hitting the putt hard enough to get it past the hole, we often knock it beyond the requisite 17 inches recommended by Pelz.

Give it the best chance

Players may console themselves with, "Well, I gave it a chance." But it wasn't the best chance.

I subscribe to the approach putting method of golf legend Bobby Jones. He believed that a putt struck too hard—a.k.a. "Never up, never in"—has only one way into the cup: through the front in the middle. But when a putt "dies at the hole" it has four doors to enter.

The ball can go in the front, the back, or either side, wherever it intercepts the perimeter. But a ball that rolls speedily up the ramp of the lumpy doughnut must hit the front door in the middle and sometimes even that putt won't go down (it pops out as if it hit the back iron of a basketball rim).

Instead of "giving it a chance," try rolling the ball to the hole. Try to make it come to rest no more than 3 to 4 inches from the perimeter of the hole. If the ball catches any part of the hole, it will drop. And if it misses, you'll have avoided the 3- to 4-foot "knee knocker" coming back.

How do you learn to make your approach putts finish within inches of the hole? You need to get a sense of feel or touch. Try the drills that follow.

One last note—although many players try to die all their putts in the hole, I feel that on shorter putts, especially those that will travel uphill or across a relatively flat surface and are within 3 feet, you should try to strike the ball firmly enough so that when it falls into the hole it hits the cup liner that is opposite to its point of entry. You might have seen Tiger Woods practice this while knocking home a short putt for birdie. A firm stroke from a short distance will keep your putt on line.

The average golfer needs to realize that rolling a ten-footer up to the front edge of the cup is to be applauded, not sneered at. The only time I can imagine when it would be dreadfully wrong to leave a putt short is if you must sink it to win the match or the tournament or the skin.

— Harvey Penick

Practice putting the ball at different distances along the same line to the hole (*left*). On uphill putts, aim for a spot 6 to 8 inches beyond the cup (*right*). This should afford your putt enough steam to drop into the hole.

Drills

These drills will help develop the necessary feel for distance when striking approach putts.

Drill #1

Place a quarter or ball mark on the green and place your balls at three different distances of 8, 10, and 12 feet. Putt to the quarter taking two practice strokes to judge the distance and then putt. Try to stop the ball on the quarter. Your pattern should get tighter and closer to the quarter. You're now developing feel.

Drill #2

Place three balls each at distances of 10, 15, and 20 feet. After stroking each ball keep your eyes down and call out how you think the ball will finish at the hole, "short" or "long" or "perfect" (within a few inches). After getting the three balls within 3 to 4 inches, move to distances of 25, 30, and 35 feet and repeat.

Drill #3

Place a quarter or other coin 6 inches behind the hole on uphill putts of 6, 8, and 10 feet. After you've finished three putts at each distance either in the hole or within the space between the coin and the hole, move to distances of 16, 20, and 24 feet and repeat the drill.

Drill #4

From a position on the green that presents a fast, straight, downhill slope to the cup place a coin 4 feet short of the hole. From distances of 6, 12, and 18 feet, putt three balls to the coin. You should be trying to stop the ball on the coin and allowing the slope to take it down to the hole. If your putts are going past the hole, move the coin closer to you. If they are short, move the coin closer to the hole. After mastering the first set of distances, increase the distance and repeat.

No. 37

Take the putter back slowly, then accelerate

The putting stroke must be made with rhythm. The change of direction should be smooth and unforced, just as it is with the pendulum of a grandfather clock.

— *Tom Watson*

The best putters on the PGA Tour—Ben Crenshaw, Loren Roberts, Brad Faxon—have an evenness and consistency to their strokes. You don't need to add acceleration to your putting stroke because a rhythmic stroke has a slight acceleration at the bottom of the arc. It's the longest part of the arc, thus the putter head is moving slightly faster than the other part of the stroke. So there's no need to speed up the stroke.

The best putters also apply consistent hand pressure throughout the stroke. They don't tighten the grip at impact. A change in hand pressure also creates problems with distance control and keeping the putter square.

My image for the proper stroke is that of a wrecking ball crashing into the back of the ball—this is the kind of energy necessary for striking a putt.

I never tell myself to hit the putt. I am always trying to get the swing of the putter to roll the ball even if I am trying to roll the ball over only one time.

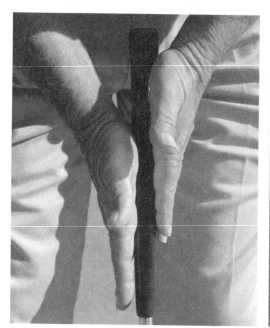 

A good pendulum stroke starts with a proper grip, palms opposing each other and parallel with the clubface (*left*). Use the image of the pendulum stroke to help you get to the proper finishing position and hold it (*right*).

LAWS OF THE LAND

Here are some valuable guidelines for behaving on the green, like Emily Post points of etiquette.

1. When all players in the group have completed play on a hole, repair any damage to the putting green caused by golf shoes.

2. On entering the green, fix ball marks (yours and any others you find close by).

3. Avoid stepping on the putting lines of others.

4. When another player is putting, don't stand in his or her line of direct or peripheral vision.

5. When retrieving a holed putt, do not flip the ball from the cup with your putter (this can damage the edge of the cup).

6. If you're tending the flag, don't stand near the hole or on an extension of the line behind the hole (this avoids the situation in which the putt goes beyond the hole and the second putt must then be rolled back over your footprints). Hold the flag so it does not flap in the breeze.

If my aiming spot for distance is as little as one-half turn from the ball's resting spot, I still contact the ball with a positive stroke and then let the slope take the ball down to the cup. If you try to simply tap the putt, your stroke will decelerate. When this occurs, you'll manipulate your hands, causing them to open or close the putter face. In most cases, you'll open up the putter face and push the putt.

The aiming spot for a very fast downhill putt can be as little as one-half turn from the ball's resting spot.

There is no tragedy in missing a putt, no matter how short. We have all erred in this respect. Short putts are missed because it is not physically possible to make the little ball travel over uncertain ground for three or four feet with any degree of regularity.

— Walter Hagen

Drill

Set up for a practice stroke and close your eyes. Make a relaxed pendulum stroke back and through, holding the completion of the stroke for two counts. Concentrate on keeping your hand pressure constant and equal. Try to sense or feel the stroke as a uniform pendulum motion. Now set up to the ball, close your eyes, make your stroke, and call out "long," "short," or "perfect."

No. 38

Putt with your shoulders

The proper putting stroke cannot be contrived or manipulated with the hands—it must be natural.

— Ben Crenshaw

This is another technique that—when followed literally—eliminates sensitivity and feel. When you concentrate on rocking your shoulders to feel the distance to the hole you still have to correlate this feeling with that of your hands, which must move the putter along the target line.

This is good advice for eliminating wobbly hands and wrists and establishing the correct speed and pace of the stroke. But no matter how you putt, or what part of the body you concentrate on, the feel of the stroke—gauging of the backswing and follow-through—is accomplished through the hands and fingers that grip the putter.

Imagine tossing a rolled-up piece of paper in the wastebasket. Your sense where to toss is with your eyes. Then you toss with your hand as your wrist relaxes and responds. Putting is the same. As you stroke or roll the ball with your hands, your shoulders rock and respond. You can reverse this, letting the shoulders rock to move the hands if you maintain feel. Find out which way you putt better, rolling the ball with your hands, or stroking with your shoulders.

The chief reaction among amateurs to poor putting, it seems to me, is exasperation, combined with a sort of vague hope that, by some kind of mini-miracle, it will all have gotten better by the next time they play.

— Jack Nicklaus

The ideal spot with which to contact the ball is with the center of the putter head meeting the center—or equator—of the ball. When you catch the ball off center you cause it to either bound in the air (contact on the upswing) or rebound off the turf (contact on the downswing). Poor contact results in loss of speed, control, and distance.

Beating the yips

Yips come from the golfer's inability to gain neuromuscular control, often brought on by anxiety. This anxiety can literally lock a golfer's muscles in place—not a pretty sight. The player wants to move the club back but his or her hands and arms act as if they're in a vise. The player freezes.

Another disastrous form of the yips occurs when the player makes a smooth takeaway but then tenses up at impact and stabs at the ball.

The yips can be conquered, and the place to start is with a new attitude. Fear, which brings on the anxiety, is the result of thinking too much about the results of what you're about to do. So don't let your mind wander to the outcome of the putt. Instead, concentrate on the execution of the putt and how you are going to hit it. Look at each putt as an opportunity for success and forget about the ones you missed. They're gone and can't be gotten back. As Ben Hogan said, "The most important shot in golf is your next one."

Also remember, you can control the read of the green, the aim of the putter head, and rolling the ball the correct distance, but you cannot make the ball go in the hole. Yips mostly start by trying to move the putter in an exactly straight line. Forget it—free up and focus on rolling the ball the right distance.

Adopt a way to focus and eliminate tension. Try this preputt routine. It will ritualize your putting setup, synchronize your stroke, and put rhythm (while reducing tension) in your routine.

1. Take two practice strokes looking at the hole, asking yourself if the pendulum you're envisioning (and practicing) will roll the ball to the target. Here is where your mind, aided by what your eyes see, must match the appropriate length of the stroke with the distance the ball must roll.
2. Aim your putter face on your intended starting line of the putt.
3. Set your feet and body parallel to your intended line.

Take two practice strokes looking at the hole (1), aim the putter and swivel your head (2) to double check your aim. As your eyes return to the ball, make your stroke (3, 4).

4. Double check the aim of the putter head with your eyes, looking first to the ball and then to the target. Shift your eyes or swivel your head, but do not rise up.

5. As your eyes return to the ball, make your stroke for distance. This entire routine should take less than 10 seconds.

Drill

Practice putting with your right hand only, left hand only, and with two hands—each with your eyes closed. Notice with one hand only you have to allow the putter head time to swing. If you rush the forward swing, you get poor contact and control. Try to develop a sense from where your feel of rolling the ball is derived. Is it from your right hand? Left hand? Or both hands? Or is it emanating from the overall pendulum motion itself?

No. 39

Swing the putter straight back and straight through

After you stroke a putt, the only thing you can do is listen for it to fall in. You're not going to gain anything by peeking.

— *Dr. Cary Middlecoff*

THE MENTAL GAME

All the great players know that one mental key has a limited lifespan, usually not lasting more than a round or two before it begins to cycle a new problem. According to Arnold Palmer, who is known for having more than 3,000 putters, he had almost as many keys. Here are his thoughts.

Key thoughts often work wonders for one round but then lose their potency if you persevere with them, and for obvious reasons. If you get a fixation about the back of your left hand (in putting, such as remembering "Keep the back of the left hand moving along the target line."), pretty soon you will transfer the responsibility for the stroke from the master hand to the left hand, and your putting will go to pot. I have used many key thoughts, and my policy was always to choose some detail of the stroke which I knew to be an important element in a good swing. So, one day I might concentrate on a light grip, switching to a steady head over the ball for the next round.

In the course of time, however, I made what seemed to be a most curious discovery: the key thought for the day need not be a vital component of the stroke. I remember, by visualizing the line and strength of my intended putt, taking my address, and then giving my full attention to the task of making an anagram from the name of my playing companions. A name like Weiskopf can keep the attention truly occupied.

Arnold Palmer came to a great realization. The elements to putting that he mulled over each day include: (1) reading the green, (2) choosing a line to start the ball on its way, (3) aiming the putter head, (4) moving the putter head directly into the back of the ball with solid contact, and (5) rolling the ball at the proper speed. However, your attention should never waiver from seeing the roll of the ball and stroking it the right distance with feel.

The notion that to hit a putt on line you must move the putter back and through precisely along the target line is incorrect. The putting stroke is actually a miniature swing arc. On a very short putt, the blade will stay almost exactly along the target line. The stroke needs only a short arc to give the ball the energy necessary to drive it up to and into the hole. However, on a longer putt, the putter head will naturally swing back slightly inside the target line—much the same way a clubhead moves inside the target line on a

The notion that to hit or putt on line you must move the putter back and through precisely along the target line is incorrect. As the stroke lengthens, the putter head will naturally swing back slightly inside the target line (2).

regular swing. On the return to the ball, the putter moves out and back on the line and meets the ball squarely. As the putter follows through, it comes up and slightly to the inside.

However, most players tend to put too much emphasis on trying to keep the putter head moving down the line after impact. You have to be careful here. If you exaggerate the follow-through you tend to shove the putter to the right. Don't force the putter to stay on the target line. Let the putter swing directly and naturally back and into the ball. Logic would tell you that you apply most of your directional sense as you move the putter away from and back into the ball. Once the ball has been struck by the putter head it's gone (its path now determined) and where the putter head goes after impact has no influence on the ball. Here is where you cultivate getting the clubface square to the target line and delivering the clubhead into the back of the ball.

Check your eye alignment

The eyes play a critical role in the art of putting. Here is an exercise to make sure your eyes are properly positioned.

Address the ball with your putter. While keeping the putter in place with your left hand take a ball in your right hand and raise it to a point directly between your eyes. Now drop the ball. Its landing point should reveal where your eyes are positioned in relation to the ball you are putting. The preferred position is along the target line directly over the ball or slightly behind it with your eyes along a backward extension of the target line. It is also okay if your eyes are slightly inside the target line with eyes forming a line parallel to the target line. But your eyes should never be outside the ball.

I have never seen a pocket billiards player lose his stroke. He's not thinking about his stroke. He's thinking about what's in front of him, as athletes in other sports do. His concern is moving the cue ball to a certain point with a certain amount of speed, not how he's holding the darn cue stick.

— Roger Maltbie

No. 40

Never move during the putting stroke

The majority treats the hole as a place more difficult to get into than it really is. The hole is pretty big, and from all distances is capable of catching a ball going at a fair pace. Many more putts would go in if players credited holes with a little of that catching power which they really possess.

— Sir Walter Simpson

On putts of considerable length—more than 30 feet—you will make a better stroke if you move ever so slightly.

Good advice, up to a point. The point being when we're talking about swaying, which is a "no-no" anytime you've got a flat stick in your hand. It's certainly advisable that when hitting short and medium-length putts you should keep the lower body quiet, or reasonably still.

However, on putts of greater length—more than 30 feet—you will make a better stroke if you let your weight move ever so slightly from side to side. This is not an out-and-out weight shift (as the weight is loaded onto the right side in the swing) but a nearly imperceptible movement to the back instep on the backstroke and to the left foot on the stroke and follow through. You need to tap into some of your athleticism on long putts, and a robotic bottom half of your body will negate this. The rhythmic flow of weight allows for your body to rotate as the putter moves freely and naturally into the shot. This slight movement actually gives you better control of the stroke, as the arms and hands will not have to compensate beyond their natural movements. Without this slight body movement the arms and hands tend to compensate, responding to the brain's message, "More power, more power," as the arms and hands make their way through the ball. It will eliminate any last-minute wrist action to make sure that you "get the ball there."

Another technique that will help you on longer putts is to let your head and eyes release. The finish of the long putting stroke should have the weight

TROUBLESHOOTING A PUSH

If you are consistently hitting your putts to the right—pushing—try this test to discover the cause of the problem. Place two tees approximately 6 inches behind the ball equidistant from the target line (the space must be at least an inch wider than the blade of your putter so it can squeeze through). Make a backstroke. If the heel of the putter catches the inside tee, you're approaching the ball with an inside-out stroke. This will knock the ball off its intended line to the right.

To fix it, work on your setup, making sure that your hands are under your shoulders. If the ball still goes to the right, it's likely that your arms are accelerating too much on the through swing.

Get a sense in the backswing of the clubface looking more at the ball going away and let the clubhead fall into the ball. Maintain a sense of pendulum action as you also feel the clubface move more directly away from the ball and more squarely into it.

slightly on the front foot, the chest facing more toward the target, the hands and putter in front of the chest, and the head rotated toward the target with the eyes naturally following the roll of the ball.

GLOSSARY

address The golfer's position when preparing to strike the ball just before beginning the backswing.

alignment The aiming of your body (your feet, knees, hips, and shoulders) and the clubface at address. Specifically, *alignment* refers to the aiming of the clubface, your feet, knees, hips and shoulders.

angle of approach There are two angles of approach to consider in golf. The first is the *angle* at which you bring the clubhead down toward the ball. The second is the *angle* from which you approach the green. There is no variance in the angle of approach on most par threes unless there are multiple tees along multiple lines to the green.

athletic position When you stand feet slightly more than shoulder-width apart, the back of the neck and head aligned with the spine, legs slightly angled with a break at the knees and your weight balanced over the legs so that you can easily control any movements of the body, you are in the athletic position. A basketball player guarding on defense, a baseball batter awaiting a pitch, a linebacker poised for the next play, a tennis player anticipating the next serve—these athletes are in the athletic position for their respective sports.

backswing The *backswing* is the part of the swing that begins when the clubhead and body start to move and turn away from the ball. When the backswing ends is not quite so clear, because during the transition from the backswing to the forward swing (downswing), the clubhead is still moving back while the hips and lower body have started toward the target.

ball flight The action of your ball in the air is its *ball flight*. Many things influence the ball's flight, but the most significant factor is the angle of the clubface at impact.

ball position When you take your address position, the ball's relationship to your feet is known as the *ball position*. If the ball is closer to your front foot than your back foot, it's forward. If it's closer to your back foot, it's back. If the ball is equidistant from your two feet, it's middle. Your ball position varies depending on what type of shot you're playing.

bent A finely textured strain of grass used for putting greens and fairways.

Bermuda Coarser than bent grass, Bermuda is typically used in fairways as well as greens in hot, humid climates. The coarser Bermuda grain can affect the line of a putt and needs to be taken into account.

casting from the top This is something you definitely don't want to do. If someone tells you, "You're *casting from the top,*" they mean that you are beginning your downswing with a lazy arm swing, including a premature uncocking of the wrists, which can lead only to a weak slap at the ball.

center-shafted A club with the shaft attached some distance from the heel of the clubhead. Such clubs are not legal under the rules of golf, except for putters.

choke down or **choke up** Whether you *choke down* or *choke up,* you're holding the club with your hands placed lower than the top of the club. It makes more sense to say you choke down because you are lowering your hands on the club and, in golf, the club is at a downward angle. However, some prefer to say choke up because that's the baseball term for when you move your hands away from the base of the bat's handle. In baseball, you always choke up because you hold the bat upright.

clear the left side When you hear someone say that a golfer *clears the left side,* it simply means he or she turns completely through the ball at impact.

closed Your stance is *closed* if your left foot is closer to the target line than your right foot. Your clubface is *closed* if it is aimed left of the target at either address or impact.

clubhead The part of the club attached to the end of the shaft, designed and weighted to hit the ball various distances and at various trajectories.

coil During your backswing when your upper body turns around the resistance of your lower body, you are creating *coil.* Swingologists speak reverently of coil, for it is the source of power that, when unleashed in the downswing, results in a terrifying collision of clubface and ball at impact.

decelerate When you putt, the idea is to keep the putter moving through the ball at a consistent speed. Sometimes, however, a player slows down the clubhead due to uncertainty. When you slow down the motion of the club in this manner, you are *decelerating* the club, which typically causes it to twist. That's not good.

delayed hit When the wrists stay fully cocked until very late in the downswing, it's sometimes referred to as a *delayed hit.* It's a silly term, since there's nothing delayed about a delayed hit—it's actually a perfectly timed swing.

dip If you have a *dip* in your swing, it just means you lower yourself to the ball a little bit through impact. Don't sweat it, it's no big deal.

divot The scar left on the ground when a golf club hits beneath the ball and excavates some turf. Divot is actually a Scottish word for a piece of turf. Remember to repair your divots.

downswing That part of the golf swing that begins at the top of the backswing and ends with ball contact.

draw A controlled shot that moves from right to left in the air.

duck hook A hook is a shot that curves sharply from right to left. A *duck hook* is a shot that appears to have been shot out of the sky by a skeet shooter, airborne one second, plummeting to earth the next. It's an ugly shot, so called because the ball appears to duck to the ground in a hurry—and so do the people playing with you. The good news is there's no such thing as a duck slice.

explosion or **explosion shot** A full-swing shot used in the sand to make the ball "explode" upward out of the bunker.

extension This term refers to the idea that your arms should be fully stretched or fully extended at impact and just beyond impact.

face The part of the clubhead designed to contact the ball. The angle of the *face* at impact affects the direction and trajectory of the ball in flight. On all clubs except the putter, the face is where the scoring lines (grooves) are located.

fade An intentional shot that curves from left to right. The difference between a *fade* and a slice, which also curves from left to right, is that a slice curves significantly more and typically beyond a predictable amount. The word *fade* refers to both the shot in flight and the act of hitting the shot.

fairway wood A club with a larger head than an iron, used for longer-distance shots from the fairway.

firm left side A swing mechanics expression that describes a straight vertical line along the left side of the body at impact, with the left leg and left side of the torso braced for the collision at impact. A player who achieves this position is said to be hitting against a *firm left side*.

flange The bottom part of the iron clubhead that projects backward from the leading edge of the clubface. The flange on a sand wedge is somewhat larger than on other clubs, which prevents the club from digging in too deeply into the sand.

flat When your swing is *flat*, it means that the plane of it (the angle at which the club swings around your body) is low or close to the ground, much like Lee Trevino's. Your backswing would be *flat*, but not your follow-through.

flex Refers to the relative flexibility or stiffness of the shaft of a golf club. Today's clubs come in a range of flexes, from extra stiff to highly flexible.

flying right elbow A swing mechanic's term used to describe a right elbow that does not stay close to the body, which is generally accepted as conventional in a proper swing. While it is not considered typical, many great players, including Jack Nicklaus and Miller Barber, have played with a *flying right elbow*.

follow-through That part of the golf swing that occurs after contact is made with the ball. A good follow-through is an important part of an effective golf swing.

grain The angle of grass on or around a green, which a player must take into account when putting and chipping.

green The putting surface. Also used to indicate the whole course, which is why course superintendents are called greenskeepers.

grip The position of the hands and fingers on the shaft.

ground To settle the head of a club into the playing surface around the ball. Clubs cannot be ground in a bunker.

heel The area of the clubface directly beneath the shaft.

hitting it thin If you contact the ball with the bottom of the clubface (last two grooves at the bottom) or hit the ball with the leading edge of the clubface, you've "hit it thin." This usually comes from moving up and out of the swing too soon or moving the body too far ahead of the ball in the downswing and through swing.

hood A term that describes the tilting forward of the clubhead, which reduces the effective loft of the club. To *hood* the club, you can do one of two things: move your hands farther ahead of the ball or move the ball farther back in your stance. You might choose to hood the club if you wish to pick up a few extra yards with a given club or if you wanted to hit the ball on a lower trajectory than is typical for the selected club.

hook A shot that, in general, curves out of control from right to left. The flight of the ball is described as a *hook*, as is the act of hitting it. There is such a thing as a controlled hook—a severely bending shot played to go around an obstacle such as a tree. If you hit a lot of hooks, you're a *hooker*.

hosel The part of the clubhead, particularly on irons, that acts as a receptacle for the shaft. The *hosel* is the part of the club that contacts the ball to create a shank. Some players refer to a shank as a hosel shot or a hosel job.

impact When the clubhead collides with the ball at the bottom of the swing, that's *impact*. In swing talk, it's described as the *impact position*.

interlocking grip One of the two basic methods for gripping the club is the *interlocking grip*, the distinguishing feature of which is the left pinkie finger interlocking with the right index finger. Most top-level players do not use the interlocking grip; however, Jack Nicklaus and Tiger Woods are two very notable exceptions.

iron An iron, as distinguished from a *wood*, is any club from a 1-iron to a wedge. Players who use an iron off the tee are willing to sacrifice distance for greater accuracy.

lag putt A long putt that comes up just short of the hole, within makeable range.

lie A lie can refer to the position of the golf ball at rest on the ground and is usually described either as a good lie or a bad lie. As a verb it is used when asking or stating how many shots a player has taken to a certain point on a hole, as in "How many do you lie?" or as an answer, "I'm lying three."

line On the green, the line is an imaginary line from the ball to the hole. From tee to green, or through the green, the line is an imaginary line in the fairway running from the tee to the hole. It's basically where a golfer wants the ball to go.

lip The edge of the cup or hole. Putts are said to lip out when they fail to drop in the hole after skirting the lip of the cup.

loft The loft of the club is the property that lifts the ball into the air. It's the angle at which the clubface leans away from the target. Also, when you hit a ball high into the air, you could say you played a *lofted* shot. Any club designed to hit such a shot, roughly from the 7 iron through the wedges, can be called a *lofted* club.

long irons Those irons that are used primarily for distance, as opposed to the short irons that are used for accuracy. Long irons are generally 1 through 3 irons, middle irons are 4 through 6 irons, and short irons include 7 through 9 irons and wedges.

mallet or **mallet-head** A type of putter with a wider and heavier head than a blade putter. They come in many variations and styles.

mid-iron Refers to one of three types of clubs: an iron, used in the nineteenth and early twentieth centuries, with somewhat more loft than a driving iron; a 2 iron; or the middle irons (4 through 6 irons) in between the long and short irons.

off line A shot that is off target is said to *off line*.

open stance An open stance is one where the golfer moves his or her forward foot back from the line of play. Open stances are favored for shorter shots requiring greater loft and accuracy, such as wedge shots, and when the player wants to fade the ball from left to right (for a right-handed player).

outside-in swing A swing that, through impact, moves from outside an imaginary line going straight back from the ball to inside that line after impact.

over the top An expression that refers to the act of the club tipping forward of the shoulders, in relation to the ball, at the beginning of the downswing, typically the result of the upper body improperly taking the lead in initiating the downswing. If you come *over the top* in your swing, you've got big problems.

overlapping grip A way of holding the golf club so that the little finger of the right hand overlaps the space between the forefinger and the second finger of the left hand (for a right-handed player). Also known as the *Vardon grip*.

pause at the top In a swing with nice tempo, there is a moment at the top of the player's swing in which the club is moving neither back nor down—it is motionless for just a split second, giving the lower body a chance to begin its downward motion. This moment of suspended animation is the *pause at the top*. You can see it expertly exaggerated in the swing of Nancy Lopez or Bob Murphy.

pitching wedge A pitching wedge is distinguished from a sand wedge by less of an angle on the clubface, less weight, and a small flange projecting backward from the face. Players typically use a pitching wedge around the green. A full swing with a pitching wedge can cause the ball to travel 100 yards or more.

pivot Refers to the rotation of the body, especially the shoulders, upper body, and hips, during the golf swing. Used as both a noun and a verb.

pronate A physiological term referring to the turning of the wrists from a palm-upward position to a palm-downward position.

pull-hook A *pull-hook* is a shot that starts out like a pull (flying on a straight line but left of the target) and evolves into a hook (a shot that curves from right to left).

push A shot that is off line to the right (for a right-handed player). The opposite of a pull. Also used as a verb, meaning to make the ball go to the right of the intended line.

putt A shot made on the green with a putter, originally from the Scottish term meaning to push gently or nudge. When tabulating the number of putts, only those shots made on the putting surface are counted; shots made with a putter from off the putting surface are not considered putts.

putter The club used for putting on the green.

reverse C A follow-through position in which the body loosely forms a *reverse C*. Once considered standard, this position is no longer espoused by swingologists due to the immense amount of strain it places on the back.

reverse overlap grip Perhaps the most common grip for putting, the *reverse overlap grip* places the left index finger over the first two or three fingers on the right hand, depending upon the player's preference.

reverse pivot Two of the ugliest words in golf, a *reverse pivot* is what occurs when you shift your weight toward the target in the backswing, as opposed to away from the target (the generally accepted technique).

rotation The twisting motion of the arms during the swing is the *rotation*.

setup position The address position is sometimes referred to as the *setup position*. The term is used to describe a player's position just prior to the start of the actual swing. In the lexicon of swing mechanics, the setup position is considered part of the swing even though the club hasn't started away from the ball. The basics of the *setup position* for a normal shot would be the clubface aimed at target and the feet, knees, hips, and shoulders aimed along a line parallel to the target line. The setup position would also include the grip, ball position, and posture the player uses.

shaft or **clubshaft** The long part of the club that connects the grip with the club head. Players may choose from shafts made of different materials, such as titanium, steel, or graphite, and of differing flexibility.

short irons Those irons that are used primarily for accuracy, as opposed to the long irons that are used for distance. Short irons include 7 through 9 irons and wedges.

slice An out-of-control shot moving from left to right is a *slice*. Hit this type of shot frequently and you're a *slicer*.

snap hook A shot that breaks off sharply to the left soon after being struck is a *snap hook*. It's the same as a duck hook.

sole The bottom surface of an iron or wood that generally rests on the ground when addressing the ball.

square When the lead edge of the club is pointed directly at the target at impact, you've achieved the ultimate goal of all golfers—a *square* clubface and a straight shot. Also, while you're taking your address position, your body is *square* to the target line if your feet, knees, hips, and shoulders are parallel to the target line. In the same position, the clubface is *square* if the lead edge is aimed directly at the target.

stance Refers to the position of the golfer's body when addressing the ball, expecially the feet in relation to the intended line of flight.

supinate A physiological term meaning to rotate the wrists so that the palms face upward.

sway Lateral movement of the hips outside the internal base created by the feet and legs.

sweep The action of picking the ball off the ground with a fairway wood, thereby avoiding solid contact with the ground, is known as *sweeping the ball*.

sweet spot or **sweetspot** That part of the clubface where it is most desirable to make contact with the ball.

swing Refers to the entire act of hitting the ball, including taking the club away from the ball, the backswing, the downswing, and the follow-through. Golfers who are "working on their swing" are trying to improve their ability to hit the ball in a consistent fashion.

takeaway The initial phase of the backswing, beginning when the club starts back from the ball and ending when it begins to move upward, is known as the *takeaway*. The term refers to the idea of taking the club away from the ball.

tempo Refers to the pace and timing, or rhythm, of a player's golf swing.

thin To hit the ball thin means to catch the ball slightly above center.

toe The end of the clubhead, opposite the heel, that is farthest from the shaft.

torque In golf, refers to the tendency of the club to twist on impact.

uncock Your wrists should cock early in your backswing and stay that way almost until the point that your arms return to the front of your body. At his point, the weight of the clubhead begins to *uncock*, or straighten, your wrists.

V The angles formed by your thumbs and forefingers when you grip the club are known as the *V*s because of the resemblance these angles bear to the letter V. The location of these Vs is one way of determining the position of the hands on the club. In a neutral grip, the Vs point to their respective shoulders.

Vardon grip Same as *overlapping grip*. Named after six-time British Open winner Harry Vardon, who developed the grip to compensate for the slimmer handles of the hickory-shafted clubs that replaced the thicker-shafted clubs around the beginning of the twentieth century.

waggle Some players utilize a waggle to prevent the onset of tension before they begin their backswing and to rehearse their takeaway. The *waggle* is a loose movement of the clubhead back and forth behind the ball immediately preceding the takeaway. The *waggle* is usually made by flipping the wrists back and forth, although some players who are concentrating on making a one-piece takeaway make a more stiff-armed waggle.

Index